P9-DCP-156

Winter 1999 Edition

COLLECTOR'S
VALUE GUIDE™
Ty® Beanie Babies®

Contents

Ty® Beanie Babies®

BEANIE BABIES®, BEANIE BUDDIES®, Ty® and the Ty Heart Logo® are registered trademarks of Ty Inc. BEANIE™, BEANIES™, PILLOW PALS™, ATTIC TREASURES™ and the individual names of each plush animal depicted in this publication are also trademarks of Ty Inc. The plush animals depicted in this publication are the copyrighted property of Ty Inc., and all photographs of Ty Inc.'s products in this publication are used by permission of Ty Inc. ©1998, Ty Inc. The poems associated with Ty Inc.'s BEANIE BABIES plush animals are also the copyrighted property of Ty Inc., and any reproduction of such poems in this publication is with the permission of Ty Inc.

The Collector's Value Guide™ is not sponsored or endorsed by, or otherwise affiliated with Ty Inc. Any opinions expressed are solely those of the authors, and do not necessarily reflect those of Ty Inc. All Copyrights and Trademarks of Ty Inc. are used by permission. All rights reserved.

Front cover foreground (left to right): "1998 Holiday Teddy™" & "Zero™" – *Beanie Babies®*
Front cover background (left to right): "Teddy™" – *Beanie Buddies®*, "Teddy™" (cranberry) –
Beanie Babies®, "Humphrey™" – *Beanie Buddies®*, "Humphrey™" –
Beanie Babies®, "Beak™" – *Beanie Babies®*, "Beak™" – *Beanie Buddies®*
Back cover (left to right): "Beak™" – *Beanie Babies®*, "Quackers™" – *Beanie Buddies®*, "Quackers™" –
Beanie Babies®, "Wise™" – *Beanie Babies®*, "Quacks™" – *Teenie Beanie Babies™*

Managing Editor:	Jeff Mahony	Art Director:	Joe T. Nguyen
	jeff@collectorspub.com		*joe@collectorspub.com*
Associate Editors:	Melissa A. Bennett	Production Supervisor:	Scott Sierakowski
	Jan Cronan	Staff Artists:	Lance Doyle
	Gia C. Manalio		Kimberly Eastman
Contributing Editor:	Mike Micciulla		Ryan Falis
Editorial Assistants:	Jennifer Filipek		David Ten Eyck
	K. Nicole LeGard		
	Ren Messina		
	Joan C. Wheal		
Research Assistant:	Steven Shinkaruk		

ISBN 1-888914-37-8

COLLECTOR'S VALUE GUIDE™ is a trademark of Collectors' Publishing Co., Inc.
Copyright © by Collectors' Publishing Co., Inc. 1998.
All rights reserved. No part of this book may be reproduced or transmitted in any form or by any means, electronic or mechanical, including photocopying, recording, or by any information storage or retrieval system, without the written permission of the publisher.

COLLECTORS' PUBLISHING CO., INC.
598 Pomeroy Avenue
Meriden, CT 06450
www.collectorspub.com
(check out our web site's exciting new look coming in December 1998)

*W*elcome to the Winter 1999 edition of the Collector's Value Guide™ to Ty® Beanie Babies®! While no one expected the cute little beanbag animals who were introduced as toys to become the hottest collectible in years, as the years go on, the *Beanie Babies®* craze continues to create excitement! Both new and experienced collectors have lots of questions about this unique line. A need for accurate, detailed information led to this guide, a fun-filled way to learn about your collection, because even serious collectors should have fun with their collections. Inside these pages, you will find:

 New September Releases And Retirements

Large Color Photos Of All The *Beanie Babies*, Including *Teenie Beanie Babies*™ And Ty's Newest Line: *Beanie Buddies*®

An In-Depth Look At Variations, Including Detailed Photos

Up-To-Date Secondary Market Values For Each Generation Tag

Comprehensive Information About Every Piece

A Look At Sports Promotion *Beanie Babies*, Their Commemorative Cards And Values

The Top Ten Most Valuable *Beanie Babies*

An Examination Of Swing Tags And Tush Tags

Fun And Games

An Overview Of Other Ty® Plush Animals

The Latest Winners Of Collectors' Publishing's Dream Beanie Contest

*C*razes come and go – almost everyone remembers the Cabbage Patch dolls and Tickle Me Elmo. But unlike other fads that fade out as quickly as they appear, *Beanie Babies* have endured despite all those original predictions that they would never survive more than one season. All over the country (and most other parts of the world) fans of all ages of those cute and cuddly beanbag toys can be found camping out in anticipation of stores opening and gathering at conventions to enhance and discuss their collections.

But let's not forget how the line was started...

NOT SO LONG AGO, IN A PLACE NOT SO FAR AWAY . . .

H. Ty Warner and his company, Ty Inc., have been producing under-stuffed, handmade plush animals since the mid-1980s. When Warner had the idea to create beanbag animals to introduce children to animals from all over the world, and at a price they could afford, the result was *Beanie Babies*.

Beanie Babies were introduced at a Chicago area trade fair in 1993. In 1994, Ty included the "Original Nine" *Beanie Babies* – "Chocolate," "Cubbie/Brownie," "Flash," "Legs," "Patti," "Pinchers," "Squealer," "Splash" and "Spot" – in its catalog . . . and the collecting world would never be the same.

Small retail gift shops in the Chicago area began to offer the *Beanie Babies* line and the plush animals were quickly grabbed up by children who couldn't resist the adorable toys – or their $5–$7 price tag. Soon, the market began to expand, and *Beanie Babies* were offered throughout all of America, and eventually in Canada and Great Britain as well.

That small price tag went a long way and today Ty Inc. is a multi-million dollar company. The company has had to move its facilities to accommodate its growth while introducing new product lines and expanding its current ones. However, Ty hasn't forgotten the humble quality or values with which the company started out way back when.

UNLIKE ANY BEAN I'VE EVER SEEN

And what makes these beanbag toys so irresistible? As a collectible line, *Beanie Babies* has many features which are truly unique.

There are many different types of *Beanie Babies*, made to appeal to many different types of people – a key element in the popularity of the line. However, it seems as though the bears have the largest appeal. "Glory," "Princess," "Erin" and "Fortune" are among the most popular current *Beanie Babies* and the old and new face styles of "Teddy" are among the most valuable *Beanie Babies* on the secondary market.

The red, heart-shaped swing tags that can be found on every design have become a big part of the *Beanie Babies* story as well. These swing tags, as well as the tush tags, have become just as essential as the animals to many collectors. For those interested in

---

BEANIE BABIES® ODDS & ENDS

National Media Crunch. The *Beanie Babies* phenomenon has made headlines in newspapers across the country and have been featured on countless television newscasts.

Disturbing The Peace. At gift shops all across the country, there have been arguments (sometimes even fights) between eager shoppers, which has forced many retailers to create new policies on the *Beanie Babies* buying process.

Fleece Artists. Counterfeit *Beanie Babies* have been appearing in the marketplace with subtle design and color variances and incorrect tags.

Rumor Tracker. New rumors arise every day as reports of new releases, retirements and variations can be heard daily through the *Beanie Babies* grapevine.

---

the value of their collection, the condition of the tag as well as the version (or "generation") of the tag become important factors.

And then there's the fun world of variations. Some of these "oddities" are highly sought after on the secondary market, such as the dark blue "Peanut" the elephant. Others don't command a higher monetary value, only that of the amusement kind, such as a few "Inky" the octopuses swimming around with one too little or one too many legs.

NOT JUST YOUR REGULAR BEANIE BABIES®

In April 1997, just when the popularity of *Beanie Babies* had reached a high point, the company joined forces with McDonald's to offer *Teenie Beanie Babies*, miniature versions of the cuddly collectibles as a part of a five-week Happy Meal promotion. As the event was anything but "teenie," the two giants teamed up again in 1998 for a second promotion, this one even crossing the Canadian border.

On May 18, 1997, Ty Inc. hit a home run when it first launched a series of promotional giveaways at sporting events. "Cubbie" the bear was given to 10,000 children who came to cheer on the Chicago Cubs and the event was such a success that the *Beanie Babies* sports promotions began to spill into other sporting leagues as well.

During a magical summer of 1998, two memorable moments in baseball history occurred on *Beanie Babies* days. On May 17, 1998, almost a year to the day since the first promotion, New York Yankees pitcher David Wells pitched a rare "perfect game" (with a little help from "Valentino") and on September 13, 1998, Sammy

Sosa of the Chicago Cubs hit two home runs to pass all-time greats Babe Ruth and Roger Maris for second place in the single-season home run rankings (as "Gracie" looked on from the crowd).

The birth of the Beanie Babies® Official Club™ in 1998 created new excitement to *Beanie Babies* collecting. Club members were introduced to "Clubby," a bright blue bear with a tie-dye ribbon and a club patch over his heart. This exclusive bear is a sure incentive to join the club before "Clubby" goes away.

BEANIE BABIES® SPIN THEIR OWN WEB

While the pieces in this line may seem simple enough, keeping up-to-date in the *Beanie Babies* world is not. With five different tag generations to monitor and products arriving and retiring frequently, a collector must be able to access updates immediately.

For a huge company, Ty has done virtually no advertising. Instead, the success of the line has relied heavily on word-of-mouth as well as the Internet. The most direct source of information is the Ty web site (*www.ty.com*), which had been accessed over 2 billion times at the time of this printing. The Ty web site is full of helpful information for collectors. In September, it became invaluable as Ty began a staggered retirement of members in several of its lines. This is the first time that retirements have been announced in this manner as over a period of two weeks, 13 *Beanie Babies*, six *Pillow Pals*™ and eight *Attic Treasures*™ had all been honored with this status.

The web site also includes a diary written by the "Info Beanie," who is voted into the month-long position by those who visit the site. Through these diary entries, the animals come alive, as the Info Beanie describes daily adventures with the other *Beanie Babies* and the rest of the Ty clan.

REALLY BIG BUDDIES

It was through this web site in September 1998 that mystery-minded collectors were led through a series of clues that would eventually culminate in the introduction of the newest collection to join the Ty family: the *Beanie Buddies®*. Created from "Tylon," an unique material developed by Ty Warner himself, these creatures are larger, softer versions of the *Beanie Babies,* including several retired designs. In a market full of beans, these new critters may just be the next big thing.

BEANIE BABIES® EVERYWHERE

For true *Beanie Babies* fans, Ty has produced a number of official products to complement any collection. Check with your local retailer for some of these new products from Ty.

Beanie Babies® Official
Collector's Cards

Beanie Babies® Official Collector's
Cards Binder

Official Ty® Heart Tag Protectors

1999 Daily Calendar

1999 Week-at-a-Glance Calendar

1999 Wall Calendar

With this large offering of products, it is now easy to turn your entire world into a *Beanie Babies* world.

*T*he *Beanie Babies* line has inspired the *Teenie Beanie Babies* and the *Beanie Buddies*, but these aren't the only popular plush collections offered by Ty. Long before *Beanie Babies* revolutionized the world of collectibles, another branch of the Ty family tree was enjoying a quiet but well-loved existence in the land of plush. In fact, Ty's product line now includes over 600 handmade, quality stuffed animals in six different collections. And many of these other collections are rapidly growing in popularity.

Back in 1986, H. Ty Warner established his own plush toy company, Ty Inc., in Oakbrook, Illinois after his experience with the company Dakin. Many *Beanie Babies* collectors are stunned to learn that Ty has been producing plush animals for over a decade! His humble start began with four longhaired Himalayan cats which were introduced along with a small group of stuffed pals. This group of animals, commonly referred to as *Ty Plush*, has expanded to include more than 300 pieces and is separated into five distinct categories: bears, cats, dogs, country and wildlife. Today, many of these critters are no longer available, but were taken out of production long before Ty began to use the official term "retirement."

"Large Curly"
from *Ty® Plush*

The Attic Treasures Collection™ was introduced in 1993 with 12 fully jointed bears and rabbits, designed to mirror the nostalgic, old-fashioned teddies of days gone by. In order to add variety to his own designs, Ty Warner enlisted the creative talents of teddy bear artists Ruth Fraser, Linda Harris, Nola Hart and Anne Nickles for a selected number of pieces in this new line. The line has undergone a series of changes throughout the years. In the mid-1990s, the name was changed to "Ty Collectibles" and in 1998 was changed

"Isabella"
from *Attic Treasures*™

back to *Attic Treasures*. And most notably, in mid-1996, the majority of the animals became fashion-conscious. Animals that were once naked or only wearing neck ribbons, were adorned with bloomers, dresses, overalls and sweaters.

In an effort to reach an even wider market, Ty introduced a new line in 1995 called *Pillow Pals*. While the line's cuddliness was definitely appealing to adults, these large, machine-washable, animal-shaped, pillow-like creatures were especially designed for babies and small children. The puffy pals' special features include embroidered eyes and noses (nothing which could be chewed off or swallowed by small hands and mouths), polyester filling (no small beans or pellets) and sewn-on neck ribbons. And if seeing these critters fills you with a sense of déjà vu, that's not surprising as many of these pieces resemble their *Beanie Babies* counterparts.

"Antlers" from
Pillow Pals™

By 1997, many of the older plush pieces had been making their homes in the corners of attics and on forgotten store shelves. However, riding on the coattails of their famous *Beanie Babies* cousins, these collections wearing Ty swing tags began to be noticed by savvy collectors and interest surged. Lately, the *Attic Treasures* have been attracting a great deal of attention on the secondary market. Like the *Beanie Babies*, the value of each *Attic Treasures* piece has become largely dependent on the generation of swing tag that the animal is wearing. And as more and more pieces are officially retired, one can only guess what adventures await the members of the other collections on the secondary market.

*S*eptember was a busy month for the Ty family. After retiring 13 *Beanie Babies* over a span of two weeks, Ty introduced 11 new critters (including the new employee bear announced in October) to the clan as well as a whole new line of nine *Beanie Buddies.*

It was all fun and games at the big September 30 party on the Ty web site as collectors faced the challenge of locating the names of the new *Beanie Babies* in a word search in order to access full-color photos of the new critters. Then it was time to open presents by clicking on their images in order to see full-color photos of the *Beanie Buddies.*

Here is a look at all the new guests that collectors had a chance to meet.

BEANIE BABIES®

1998 Holiday Teddy™ . . . Deck the halls with "1998 Holiday Teddy!" In anticipation of the upcoming season, this teddy is covered in holly leaves and berries and is waiting under the mistletoe for someone to kiss! Resembling a cross between the ever-popular "1997 Teddy" and "Glory," the second dated bear to join the *Beanie Babies* family is sure to bring Christmas cheer to even the biggest of scrooges.

Beak™ . . . "Beak" has travelled a long way from her exotic home to be closer to her *Beanie Babies* friends. A rather unusual looking bird, "Beak" knows how to make an impression on collectors. And if you think you're seeing double, don't worry, you are. "Beak" is the first of the *Beanie Babies* to be released simultaneously with her *Beanie Buddies* companion, also named "Beak."

Canyon™ . . . We're not "cattin' around" when we say that you're gonna love this new addition to the *Beanie Babies* family! Despite a gruff demeanor, "Canyon," the first cougar to join the clan, is just as soft and cuddly as the more domesticated members of the feline family.

Halo™ . . . This winged little guardian angel has flown straight down from heaven to love and watch over collectors everywhere. When you see this vision in white, with sparkling wings and halo, you won't be able to "bear" one more minute without this very unique and heavenly addition!

Loosy™ . . . Take a "gander" at this new addition to the *Beanie Babies* family! "Loosy" the goose has arrived, complete with a red bow, for celebrating the holiday season! So make some room in your home, this joyful bird has come to join the holiday festivities.

Pumkin'™ . . . With a grin like that, one can only wonder what this pumpkin is up to. But there's nothing to fear, with open arms like that, he's just waiting to be hugged. To help keep the spirits away, "Pumkin'" is the perfect companion while waiting for Halloween trick or treaters, as well as all year round.

Roam™ . . . Even though the days when buffalo freely roamed the ranges have ended, this little guy has survived extinction. A magnificent animal with his furry face and back, this buffalo is sure to "roam" right into the hearts of collectors. And once he gets there, there will be no more traveling for "Roam" as your love will cure his wanderlust.

Santa™ . . . Ho ho ho . . . guess who's here! Leave out the milk and cookies, because "Santa" has come to town! This jolly little elf brings his own unique gift to your collection as he is the first of his kind to join the *Beanie Babies* and most definitely the first to have a driving license (or would that be a *sledding* license).

Scorch™ . . . This bewitching creature is sure to breathe a little warmth into your heart this winter. With iridescent wings and multi-colored fur, no one is going to want to slay this dragon! As the second dragon in the collection, "Scorch" continues to bring a sense of mysticism where his retired pal "Magic" left off.

Zero™ . . . That's how much resistance you'll have to this adorable little penguin! "Zero" is a picture of holiday style in his tux – which he finds fitting attire for all seasons – and Christmas hat. As Santa's little helper and the only currently available penguin in the collection, "Zero" is all bundled up from the Arctic cold and is ready to help ring in the holiday season.

Ty Creates A New Billionaire™

In a show of appreciation for a job well done, Ty Inc. once again presented its employees with a token of its gratitude: a new *Beanie Babies* bear named "Billionaire." This special bear is made from the same fabric as the new *Beanie Buddies*. As described on the Ty web site, "Billionaire" is "a really neat shade of brown. It's two colors mixed together. He also has a dollar sign embroidered on his chest in a bright green." A special touch for collectors who are able to acquire this rare bear: Ty Warner himself signed each and every swing tag.

BEANIE BUDDIES®

With a large sense of déjà vu, collectors were introduced to the *Beanie Buddies*. However, a quick introduction this was not. Through daily entries in the Info Beanie's diary on the Ty web site during the month of September, collectors were led through a series of clues that sent "Wise" the owl on a quest to discover the truth about the strange things that were happening around Ty headquarters. On numerous occasions, "Wise" spotted strange animals sneaking around; large, unidentified footprints; clumps of fur; missing sandwiches and strange notes. Try as he might, "Wise" was unable to make heads nor tails out of these occurrences, often passing on his discoveries to collectors on-line. On the last day of the month, all was revealed at a party on the web site and the *Beanie Buddies* were finally introduced.

Mirror images of some of the *Beanie Babies*, some of which have retired, the *Beanie Buddies* have soft fur and are much larger than their counterparts. The first buddies to join the Ty family include "Beak" the kiwi, "Humphrey" the camel, "Jake" the mallard duck, "Peanut" the elephant, "Quackers" the duck, "Rover" the dog, "Stretch" the ostrich, "Teddy" the bear and "Twigs" the giraffe.

*S*eptember 1998 marked the first time in history that the *Beanie Babies* line saw staggered retirements. Whereas collectors were accustomed to seeing mass retirements every couple of months, they were surprised to find that nearly every day of the last two weeks of September led to the end of production for another one or more of their favorite animals. Here is a complete list of all of the officially retired *Beanie Babies* with their animal type and issue year:

SEPTEMBER 1998 RETIREMENTS

Bern ie™	*St. Bernard*,	1997
Blackie™	*bear*,	1994
Bruno™	*dog*,	1997
Crunch™	*shark*,	1997
Daisy™	*cow*,	1994
Puffer™	*puffin*,	1997
Ringo™	*raccoon*,	1996
Seaweed™	*otter*,	1996
Sly™	*fox*,	1996
Snort™	*bull*,	1997
Spinner™	*spider*,	1997
Stinky™	*skunk*,	1995
Wrinkles™	*bulldog*,	1996

BEANIE BABIES® RETIREMENTS

RETIRED MAY 1, 1998

Baldy™ . . . . eagle, 1997
Blizzard™ . . . . . . tiger, 1997
Bones™ . . . . dog, 1994
Ears™ . . . . rabbit, 1996
Echo™ . . . . dolphin, 1997
Floppity™ . . . . . bunny, 1997
Gracie™ . . . . swan, 1997
Happy™ . . . . hippo, 1994
Hippity™ . . . . . . bunny, 1997
Hoppity™ . . . . . . bunny, 1997
Inch™ . . . . . inchworm, 1995
Inky™ . . . . octopus, 1994
Jolly™ . . . . walrus, 1997
Lucky™ . . . . . . ladybug, 1994

Patti™ . . . . . . platypus, 1994
Peanut™ . . . . elephant, 1995
Pinchers™ . . . . lobster, 1994
Quackers™ . . . . . duck, 1994
Rover™ . . . . dog, 1996
Scottie™. Scottish terrier, 1996
Squealer™ . . . . pig, 1994
Stripes™ . . . . tiger, 1995
Twigs™ . . . . . . giraffe, 1996
Waddle™ . . . . penguin, 1995
Waves™ . . . . whale, 1997
Weenie™ . . dachshund, 1996
Ziggy™ . . . . zebra, 1995
Zip™ . . . . cat, 1995

RETIRED DECEMBER 31, 1997

1997 Teddy™ . . . bear, 1997
Bucky™ . . . . . . beaver, 1996
Cubbie™ . . . . bear, 1994
Goldie™ . . . . . goldfish, 1994
Lizzy™ . . . . lizard, 1995

Magic™ . . . . . . dragon, 1995
Nip™ . . . . cat, 1995
Snowball™ . . snowman, 1997
Spooky™ . . . . . . ghost, 1995

RETIRED OCTOBER 1, 1997

Ally™ . . . . alligator, 1994
Bessie™ . . . . cow, 1995
Flip™ . . . . cat, 1996
Hoot™ . . . . owl, 1996
Legs™ . . . . frog, 1994
Seamore™ . . . . . . seal, 1994

Speedy™ . . . . . . turtle, 1994
Spot™ . . . . dog, 1994
Tank™ . . . . . armadillo, 1996
Teddy™ (brown) . bear, 1994
Velvet™ . . . . panther, 1995

RETIRED MAY 11, 1997

Bubbles™ . . . . *fish*, 1995
Digger™ . . . . *crab*, 1994
Flash™ . . . . *dolphin*, 1994
Garcia™ . . . . *bear*, 1996
Grunt™ . . . . *razorback*, 1996

Manny™ . . . . . *manatee*, 1996
Radar™ . . . . *bat*, 1995
Sparky™ . . . *dalmatian*, 1996
Splash™ . . . . *whale*, 1994

RETIRED JANUARY 1, 1997

Chops™ . . . . *lamb*, 1996
Coral™ . . . . *fish*, 1995
Kiwi™ . . . . *toucan*, 1995
Lefty™ . . . . . . *donkey*, 1996
Libearty™ . . . . . . *bear*, 1996

Righty™ . . . . *elephant*, 1996
Sting™ . . . . . . *stingray*, 1995
Tabasco™ . . . . *bull*, 1995
Tusk™ . . . . *walrus*, 1995

RETIRED JUNE 15, 1996

Bronty™. *brontosaurus*, 1995
Bumble™ . . . . *bee*, 1995
Caw™ . . . . *crow*, 1995

Flutter™ . . . *butterfly*, 1995
Rex™ . . *tyrannosaurus*, 1995
Steg™ . . . *stegosaurus*, 1995

RETIRED JANUARY 7, 1996

Chilly™ . . . . *polar bear*, 1994
Peking™ . . . . *panda*, 1994
Teddy™
(cranberry) . . . . . *bear*, 1994
Teddy™ (jade) . . *bear*, 1994

Teddy™
(magenta) . . . . . . *bear*, 1994
Teddy™ (teal) . . . *bear*, 1994
Teddy™ (violet) . *bear*, 1994
Web™ . . . . *spider*, 1994

RETIRED JUNE 15, 1995

Humphrey™ . . . . *camel*, 1994
Slither™ . . . . . . *snake*, 1994

Trap™ . . . . *mouse*, 1994

RETIRED BUT NOT EXACTLY TAKING IT EASY

Brownie™
Doodle™
Nana™

These members of the *Beanie Babies* family underwent name changes at some point during production. While they are no longer available with their original names, they were never officially "retired." Because of their unique status, these pieces are highly coveted members of the *Beanie Babies* community.

Ty® Swing Tags And Tush Tags

$\mathscr{B}$efore anyone realized that *Beanie Babies* would join the world of collectibles and that their tags would play such an important role in determining their value, people routinely snipped and tossed the red paper heart tags away before the toy was given to a child. Besides, that's what it says on the tag's instructions!

Now, everyone who deals with these beanbag critters is aware of the importance of these swing tags. Both the paper heart-shaped tag (attached near the animal's head) and cloth tush tag (attached near the animal's posterior) should be present and in perfect, like-new condition in order to attain the highest price on the secondary market.

Both the swing and tush tags have been produced in generations which reflect the time period in which the particular piece was made. As a result, by determining which generation tag the animal is wearing, you can determine the approximate age of the piece. It is most often the oldest generation tag that carries the highest value on the secondary market.

Generation 1

The Beanie Babies Collection
Brownie ™ style 4010
© 1993 Ty Inc. Oakbrook, IL. USA
All Rights Reserved. Caution:
Remove this tag before giving
toy to a child. For ages 5 and up.
Handmade in Korea.
Surface
Wash.

Generation 2

The Beanie Babies Collection
© 1993 Ty Inc. Oakbrook IL. USA
All Rights Reserved. Caution:
Remove this tag before giving
toy to a child. For ages 3 and up.
Handmade in China
Surface
Wash.

Chilly ™ style 4012
to _____
from _____
with
love

BEANIE BABIES® SWING TAGS

Generation 1 (Early 1994-Mid 1994):
These tags are single red hearts with no fold and have a skinny "ty" printed on front. The animal's name, style number, reference to "The Beanie Babies Collection" and company information all appear on the back.

Generation 2 (Mid 1994-Early 1995):
The front of this tag features the same skinny "ty" logo and red heart design, but the tag opens like a book. Inside is the name and style number, a "to/from/with love" section for gift giving, refer-

ence to "The Beanie Babies Collection," plus care, cautionary and company information.

Generation 3 (Early 1995-Early 1996):

This tag is the first to feature the "puffed out" Ty logo. Inside, the information remains the same except for the addition of a trademark symbol after the word "Babies" in the collection's name and Ty's three corporate addresses.

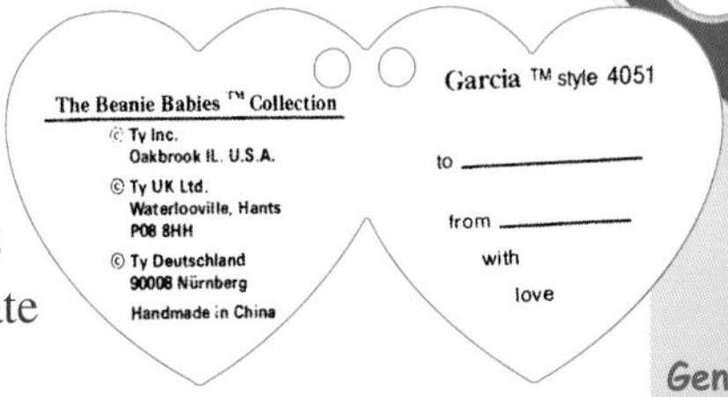

Generation 3

The Beanie Babies ™ Collection
© Ty Inc.
Oakbrook IL. U.S.A.
© Ty UK Ltd.
Waterlooville, Hants
PO8 8HH
© Ty Deutschland
90008 Nürnberg
Handmade in China

Garcia ™ style 4051
to _____
from _____
with
love

Generation 4 (Early 1996-Late 1997): The

addition of a yellow star emblazoned with the words "Original Beanie Baby" make this swing tag quite distinct from its predecessors. The inside text of the swing tag also underwent a dramatic change with the addition of the animal's birthday and poem, as well as Ty's web site address.

Generation 4

The Beanie Babies™Collection
© Ty Inc.
Oakbrook IL. U.S.A.
© Ty UK Ltd.
Fareham, Hants
PO15 5TX
© Ty Deutschland
90008 Nürnberg
Handmade in China

Doodle™ style 4171
DATE OF BIRTH : 3 - 8 - 96
Listen closely to "cock-a-doodle-doo"
What's the rooster saying to you?
Hurry, wake up sleepy head
We have lots to do, get out of bed!
Visit our web page!!!
http://www.ty.com

Generation 5 (Late 1997-Current): The out-

side of this tag is similar to the 4th generation tag, with the only difference being the typeface of "Original Beanie Baby." On the inside, the animal's birthday is written out (February 13, 1995 instead of 2-13-95), the Internet address is abbreviated and the piece's style number deleted (this information can be found as the last four digits of the UPC bar code on the back of the tag). The corporate offices of Ty UK and Ty Deutschland became collectively known as "Ty Europe" and were listed

Generation 5

The Beanie Babies Collection®
© Ty Inc.
Oakbrook, IL. U.S.A.
© Ty Europe Ltd.
Fareham, Hants
PO15 5TX, U.K
© Ty Canada
Aurora, Ontario
Handmade in China

Pinky™
DATE OF BIRTH: February 13, 1995
Pinky loves the everglades
From the hottest pink she's made
With floppy legs and big orange beak
She's the Beanie that you seek !
www.ty.com

alongside Ty USA and Ty Canada. Also, the name "Beanie Babies Collection" became registered (®).

BEANIE BABIES® TUSH TAGS

Version 1: The first *Beanie Babies* tush tags are white with black printing and list company and production information.

Version 1

Version 2: The red heart Ty logo is added to the information on the tush tag which is printed in red.

Version 3: This tag features the addition of the name of the animal below the Ty heart and "The Beanie Babies Collection™" above.

Version 2   Version 3

Version 4: This tush tag sports a small red star in the upper left-hand side of the Ty heart logo. On some tags, a clear sticker with the star was placed next to the Ty logo.

Version 5: In late 1997, these tags began to appear with a registration mark (®) after "Beanie Babies" in the collection's name and a trademark (™) after the animal's name.

Version 4   Version 5

Version 6: The most recent tush tags feature another slight change in trademark symbols. The registration mark (®) in the collection's name moved from after "Beanie Babies" to after "Collection," replacing the previous trademark. Some of the recent tush tags have also noted a change to "P.E." pellets rather than "P.V.C."

Version 6

By mid-1998, a red stamp was beginning to appear on some *Beanie Babies'* tush tags. Inside the fold, an oval containing Chinese writing with numbers can be found, indicating the factory at which the piece was produced.

*T*his section highlights the ten most valuable *Beanie Babies* as determined by their secondary market value. Since the secondary market is constantly fluctuating, the values of these *Beanie Babies* are not "set in stone," and can increase or decrease by the minute. Note that many of the pieces on this list are variations or have older swing tags (tag generations are denoted by the numbered red hearts). So, whether you're the proud owner of one of these *Beanie Babies* or are looking to add them to your collection, enjoy the following listing of those at the top of the charts, because you never know who will be next!

PEANUT™ (Dark Blue). . Market Value: ❸ – $5,300

It is estimated that only 2,000 of the dark blue elephants were produced in July 1995 before Ty changed the color to light blue. The light blue "Peanut" retired on May 1, 1998.

BROWNIE™ . . . . . . Market Value: ❶ – $4,200

One of the "Original Nine" *Beanie Babies* introduced in 1994, the name of this bear changed from "Brownie" to "Cubbie." "Cubbie" was eventually retired at the end of 1997.

NANA™ . . . . Market Value: ❸ – $4,100

"Nana" also received a name change soon after production started. You may recognize this little fellow as "Bongo" the monkey, which is currently available.

TEDDY™ (Violet, Employee Bear, No Swing Tag) . . . . . Market Value: $4,000

One of the rarest bears in the collection, "Teddy" (violet) was produced without a swing tag and given to Ty employees in recognition of their hard work and dedication to the company.

PINCHERS™
("Punchers™" Swing Tag) Market Value: ① – $3,950

Several of these lobsters were produced with a swing tag declaring their name to be "Punchers."

DERBY™ (Fine Mane) . . Market Value: ③ – $3,900

While he currently sports coarse yarn for his mane and tail, "Derby" was originally produced with a very fine and thin mane and tail, a variation that has made the older "Derby" very valuable.

TEDDY™
(Brown, Old Face) . . . . Market Value: ① – $3,100

"Teddy" originally featured a pointy snout and far apart eyes, before being redesigned. Even the brown, old face "Teddy" with a 2nd generation tag fetches a secondary market price of $2,900!

CHILLY™ . . . . Market Value: ① – $2,500

Adding to the fact that "Chilly" was only in production for just over one year, his pure white coat makes him difficult to keep clean. "Chilly" found in mint condition is nearly impossible to find!

HUMPHREY™ . . . . . . Market Value: ① – $2,450

Rejected by collectors for years for being "too unique," this brown camel is now enjoying the last laugh while avid *Beanie Babies* fans search everywhere for him!

PEKING™ . . . . Market Value: ① – $2,400

"Peking" is almost as rare as his animal counterpart, the panda. With "Peking" only in production for just over one year, *Beanie Babies* collectors rejoiced when another panda, "Fortune," was released in 1998.

*I*t's easy to determine the current value of your *Beanie Babies* collection:

1. For each *Beanie Babies* piece you own, write the price paid and date purchased in the space provided. Note: If only an estimated issue date is available, it is marked as "Est."

2. To determine the market value of your piece, first identify which swing tag is attached and write the number of its generation in the space provided. To find out which generation tag your animal has, consult the chart to the right (for more details see pages 18-20). The market value for each generation tag is listed next to the appropriate symbol. For current *Beanie Babies* with a 5th generation tag, fill in the current market value, which is usually the price you paid. Sports Promotion *Beanie Babies* are listed beginning on page 107 and are marked in the Value Guide with the appropriate symbol.

TY® TAG KEY

⑤ – 5th Generation

④ – 4th Generation

③ – 3rd Generation

② – 2nd Generation

① – 1st Generation

SPORTS PROMOTION BEANIE BABIES® KEY

- Canadian Special Olympics
- Major League Baseball
- National Basketball Association
- National Football League
- National Hockey League
- Women's National Basketball Association

3. Add the "Market Value" of each of the *Beanie Babies* you own and write the sum in the "Value Totals" box on each page. Use a pencil so you can make changes as your collection grows. Then write in your totals from each Value Guide page on page 119 and add the sums together to get the "Grand Total" of your *Beanie Babies* collection.

ON THE HUNT FOR BEANIE BABIES®

Some current *Beanie Babies* with 5th generation tags are relatively easy to find at the original retail price of $5-$7. Newly-released pieces are often sold for a "higher than retail" price at first, which levels off a bit once the supply becomes more plentiful. Other hard to find current *Beanie Babies* might sell for as much as $25-$40. Some animals are nearly impossible to find and can be sold for hundreds of dollars while still current.

In the Value Guide, all current *Beanie Babies* are labeled according to the "degree of difficulty" in finding them at the original retail price. Happy hunting!

For more Value Guide instructions, see the previous page.

DEGREE OF DIFFICULTY RATINGS

Just Released
Easy To Find
Moderate To Find
Hard To Find
Very Hard To Find
Impossible To Find

1

1997 Teddy™

Bear · #4200
Issued: October 1, 1997
Retired: December 31, 1997

Market Value:
❹-$65

Birthdate: December 25, 1996
Price Paid: $_____
Date Purchased: _____
Tag Generation: _____

Beanie Babies are special no doubt
All filled with love – inside and out
Wishes for fun times filled with joy
Ty's holiday teddy is a magical toy!

Value
Totals _____

COLLECTOR'S
VALUE GUIDE™

2

1998
Holiday Teddy™

NEW!

Bear • #4204
Issued: September 30, 1998
Current – Just Released

Market Value:
5 – $_____

Dressed in his PJ's, and ready for bed
  Hugs given, good nights said
    This little Beanie will stay close at night
      Ready for a hug at first morning light!

Birthdate: December 25, 1998
Price Paid: $_____
Date Purchased: _____
Tag Generation: _____

3

Ally™

Alligator • #4032
Issued: June 25, 1994
Retired: October 1, 1997

Market Value:
4 – $65
3 – $140
2 – $255
1 – $375

When Ally gets out of classes
  He wears a hat and dark glasses
  He plays bass in a street band
  He's the coolest gator in the land!

Birthdate: March 14, 1994
Price Paid: $_____
Date Purchased: _____
Tag Generation: _____

COLLECTOR'S
VALUE GUIDE™

Value
Totals _____

4

Ants™

Anteater • #4195
Issued: May 30, 1998
Current – Moderate To Find

Market Value:
⑤- $_____

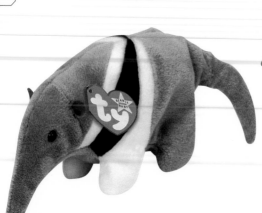

Birthdate: November 7, 1997
Price Paid: $_____
Date Purchased: _____
Tag Generation: _____

Most anteaters love to eat bugs
But this little fellow gives big hugs
He'd rather dine on apple pie
Than eat an ant or harm a fly!

5

Baldy™

Eagle • #4074
Issued: May 11, 1997
Retired: May 1, 1998

Market Value:
⑤- $22
④- $28

Birthdate: February 17, 1996
Price Paid: $_____
Date Purchased: _____
Tag Generation: _____

Hair on his head is quite scant
We suggest Baldy get a transplant
Watching over the land of the free
Hair in his eyes would make it hard to see!

Value
Totals _____

COLLECTOR'S
VALUE GUIDE™

Batty™

6

Bat · #4035
Issued: October 1, 1997
Current – Easy To Find

Market Value:
⑤- $_____
④- $25

Bats may make some people jitter
Please don't be scared of this critter
If you're lonely or have nothing to do
This Beanie Baby would love to hug you!

Birthdate: October 29, 1996
Price Paid: $_____
Date Purchased: _____
Tag Generation: _____

Beak™

7

NEW!

Kiwi · #4211
Issued: September 30, 1998
Current – Just Released

Market Value:
⑤- $_____

Isn't this just the funniest bird?
When we saw her, we said "how absurd"
Looks aren't everything, this we know
Her love for you, she's sure to show!

Birthdate: February 3, 1998
Price Paid: $_____
Date Purchased: _____
Tag Generation: _____

8

Bernie™

St. Bernard · #4109
Issued: January 1, 1997
Retired: September 22, 1998

Market Value:
- ⑤- $12
- ④- $16

Birthdate: October 3, 1996
Price Paid: $_____
Date Purchased: _____
Tag Generation: _____

This little dog can't wait to grow
To rescue people lost in the snow
Don't let him out – keep him on your shelf
He doesn't know how to rescue himself!

9

Bessie™

Cow · #4009
Issued: June 3, 1995
Retired: October 1, 1997

Market Value:
- ④- $70
- ③- $145

Birthdate: June 27, 1995
Price Paid: $_____
Date Purchased: _____
Tag Generation: _____

Bessie the cow likes to dance and sing
Because music is her favorite thing
Every night when you are counting sheep
She'll sing you a song to help you sleep!

Value
Totals _____

COLLECTOR'S
VALUE GUIDE™

SPECIAL

NEW!

Billionaire™

(exclusive Ty employee gift)

Bear • N/A

Issued: October 10, 1998

Not Available In Retail
Stores – Impossible To Find

Market Value:
Special Tag – N/E

Dedication Appearing On Special Tag
 In recognition of value and
 contributions in shipping over
 a billion dollars since Jan '98,
 I present to you this exclusive
 signed bear!

Birthdate: N/A

Price Paid: $_____

Date Purchased: _____

Tag Generation: _____

Blackie™

10

Bear • #4011

Issued: June 25, 1994

Retired: September 15, 1998

Market Value:
  ⑤ – $12
  ④ – $16
  ③ – $105
  ② – $215
  ① – $330

Living in a national park
 He only played after dark
 Then he met his friend Cubbie
 Now they play when it's sunny!

Birthdate: July 15, 1994

Price Paid: $_____

Date Purchased: _____

Tag Generation: _____

11

Blizzard™

Tiger • #4163
Issued: May 11, 1997
Retired: May 1, 1998

Market Value:
⑤- $28
④- $35

Birthdate: December 12, 1996
Price Paid: $_____
Date Purchased: _____
Tag Generation: _____

In the mountains, where it's snowy and cold
Lives a beautiful tiger, I've been told
Black and white, she's hard to compare
Of all the tigers, she is most rare!

12

Bones™

Dog • #4001
Issued: June 25, 1994
Retired: May 1, 1998

Market Value:
⑤- $22
④- $26
③- $120
②- $240
①- $335

Birthdate: January 18, 1994
Price Paid: $_____
Date Purchased: _____
Tag Generation: _____

Bones is a dog that loves to chew
Chairs and tables and a smelly old shoe
"You're so destructive" all would shout
But that all stopped, when his teeth
Fell out!

Value
Totals _____

COLLECTOR'S
VALUE GUIDE™

Bongo™

(name changed from "Nana™")

Monkey · #4067
Issued: June 3, 1995
Current – Moderate To Find

Market Value:
A. Tan Tail
   (June 95-Current)
   ❺- $_____
   ❹- $14
   ❸- $150
B. Brown Tail
   (Feb. 96–June 96)
   ❹- $70
   ❸- $145

13

B
A

Bongo the monkey lives in a tree
The happiest monkey you'll ever see
In his spare time he plays the guitar
One of these days he will be a big star!

Birthdate: August 17, 1995
Price Paid: $_____
Date Purchased: _____
Tag Generation: _____

Britannia™

(exclusive to Great Britain)

Bear · #4601
Issued: December 31, 1997
Current – Impossible To Find

Market Value
(in U.S. market):
   ❺- $500

14

Britannia the bear will sail the sea
So she can be with you and me
She's always sure to catch the tide
And wear the Union Flag with pride

Birthdate: December 15, 1997
Price Paid: $_____
Date Purchased: _____
Tag Generation: _____

COLLECTOR'S
VALUE GUIDE™

Value
Totals _____

15

Bronty™

Brontosaurus · #4085
Issued: June 3, 1995
Retired: June 15, 1996

Market Value:
 - $1,100

Birthdate: N/A

Price Paid: $_____
Date Purchased: _____
Tag Generation: _____

No Poem_____
_____
_____
_____

16

ORIGINAL
NINE

Brownie™

(name changed to "Cubbie™")

Bear · #4010
Issued: January 8, 1994
Retired: 1994

Market Value:
❶ - $4,200

Birthdate: N/A

Price Paid: $_____
Date Purchased: _____
Tag Generation: _____

No Poem_____
_____
_____
_____

Value
Totals _____

COLLECTOR'S
VALUE GUIDE™

Bruno™

Dog · #4183
Issued: December 31, 1997
Retired: September 18, 1998

Market Value:
⑤– $12

Bruno the dog thinks he's a brute
But all the other Beanies think he's cute
He growls at his tail and runs in a ring
And everyone says, "Oh, how darling!"

Birthdate: September 9, 1997
Price Paid: $_____
Date Purchased: _____
Tag Generation: _____

Bubbles™

Fish · #4078
Issued: June 3, 1995
Retired: May 11, 1997

Market Value:
④– $175
③– $235

All day long Bubbles likes to swim
She never gets tired of flapping her fins
Bubbles lived in a sea of blue
Now she is ready to come home with you!

Birthdate: July 2, 1995
Price Paid: $_____
Date Purchased: _____
Tag Generation: _____

Value
Totals _____

19

Bucky™

Beaver · #4016
Issued: January 7, 1996
Retired: December 31, 1997

Market Value:
❹ - $45
❸ - $130

Birthdate: June 8, 1995
Price Paid: $_____
Date Purchased: _____
Tag Generation: _____

Bucky's teeth are as shiny as can be
Often used for cutting trees
He hides in his dam night and day
Maybe for you he will come out and play!

20

Bumble™

Bee · #4045
Issued: June 3, 1995
Retired: June 15, 1996

Market Value:
❹ - $675
❸ - $625

Birthdate: October 16, 1995
Price Paid: $_____
Date Purchased: _____
Tag Generation: _____

Bumble the bee will not sting you
It is only love that this bee will bring you
So don't be afraid to give this bee a hug
Because Bumble the bee is a love-bug.

Value
Totals _____

COLLECTOR'S
VALUE GUIDE™

21

Canyon™

NEW!

Cougar · #4212
Issued: September 30, 1998
Current – Just Released

Market Value:
🧡-$_____

I climb rocks and really run fast
Try to catch me, it's a blast
Through the mountains, I used to roam
Now in your room, I'll call home!

Birthdate: May 29, 1998
Price Paid: $_____
Date Purchased: _____
Tag Generation: _____

22

Caw™

Crow · #4071
Issued: June 3, 1995
Retired: June 15, 1996

Market Value:
🖤-$710

No Poem_____
_____
_____

Birthdate: N/A
Price Paid: $_____
Date Purchased: _____
Tag Generation: _____

COLLECTOR'S
VALUE GUIDE™

Value
Totals _____

23

Chilly™

Polar Bear • #4012
Issued: June 25, 1994
Retired: January 7, 1996

Market Value:
❸- $2,200
❷- $2,300
❶- $2,500

Birthdate: N/A
Price Paid: $_____
Date Purchased: _____
Tag Generation: _____

No Poem_____
_____
_____
_____

24

Chip™

Cat • #4121
Issued: May 11, 1997
Current – Easy To Find

Market Value:
❺- $_____
❹- $14

Birthdate: January 26, 1996
Price Paid: $_____
Date Purchased: _____
Tag Generation: _____

Black and gold, brown and white
The shades of her coat are quite a sight
At mixing her colors she was a master
On anyone else it would be a disaster!

Value
Totals _____

COLLECTOR'S
VALUE GUIDE™

Chocolate™

Moose · #4015
Issued: January 8, 1994
Current – Easy To Find

Market Value:
- 5 - $_____
- 4 - $16
- 3 - $115
- 2 - $225
- 1 - $330

Licorice, gum and peppermint candy
This moose always has these handy
There is one more thing he likes to eat
Can you guess his favorite sweet?

Birthdate: April 27, 1993
Price Paid: $_____
Date Purchased: _____
Tag Generation: _____

Chops™

Lamb · #4019
Issued: January 7, 1996
Retired: January 1, 1997

Market Value:
- 4 - $195
- 3 - $270

Chops is a little lamb
This lamb you'll surely know
Because every path that you may take
This lamb is sure to go!

Birthdate: May 3, 1996
Price Paid: $_____
Date Purchased: _____
Tag Generation: _____

Value
Totals _____

27

Claude™

Crab · #4083
Issued: May 11, 1997
Current – Easy To Find

Market Value:
5 – $_____
4 – $16

Birthdate: September 3, 1996
Price Paid: $_____
Date Purchased: _____
Tag Generation: _____

Claude the crab paints by the sea
A famous artist he hopes to be
But the tide came in and his paints fell
Now his art is on his shell!

28

Clubby™
(exclusive to Beanie Babies®
Official Club™ members)

Bear · N/A
Issued: May 1, 1998
Current – Moderate To Find

Market Value:
5 – $_____

Birthdate: July 7, 1998
Price Paid: $_____
Date Purchased: _____
Tag Generation: _____

Wearing his club pin for all to see
He's a proud member like you and me
Made especially with you in mind
Clubby the bear is one of a kind!

PROUD

Value
Totals _____

COLLECTOR'S
VALUE GUIDE™

Congo™

Gorilla · #4160
Issued: June 15, 1996
Current – Easy To Find

Market Value:
⑤- $_____
④- $14

Black as the night and fierce is he
On the ground or in a tree
Strong and mighty as the Congo
He's related to our Bongo!

Birthdate: November 9, 1996
Price Paid: $_____
Date Purchased: _____
Tag Generation: _____

Coral™

Fish · #4079
Issued: June 3, 1995
Retired: January 1, 1997

Market Value:
④- $215
③- $300

Coral is beautiful, as you know
Made of colors in the rainbow
Whether it's pink, yellow or blue
These colors were chosen just for you!

Birthdate: March 2, 1995
Price Paid: $_____
Date Purchased: _____
Tag Generation: _____

COLLECTOR'S
VALUE GUIDE™

Value
Totals _____

31

Crunch™

Shark · #4130
Issued: January 1, 1997
Retired: September 24, 1998

Market Value:
⑤- $12
④- $15

Birthdate: January 13, 1996
Price Paid: $_____
Date Purchased: _____
Tag Generation: _____

What's for breakfast? What's for lunch?
Yum! Delicious! Munch, munch, munch!
He's eating everything by the bunch
That's the reason we named him Crunch!

32

Cubbie™

(name changed from "Brownie™")
Bear · #4010
Issued: January 8, 1994
Retired: December 31, 1997

Market Value:
⑤- $35
④- $35
③- $130
②- $245
①- $380

Birthdate: November 14, 1993
Price Paid: $_____
Date Purchased: _____
Tag Generation: _____

Cubbie used to eat crackers and honey
And what happened to him was funny
He was stung by fourteen bees
Now Cubbie eats broccoli and cheese!

Value
Totals _____

COLLECTOR'S
VALUE GUIDE™

Curly™

33

Bear · #4052
Issued: June 15, 1996
Current – Moderate To Find

Market Value:
⑤- $_____
④- $30

A bear so cute with hair that's Curly
You will love and want him surely
To this bear always be true
He will be a friend to you!

Birthdate: April 12, 1996
Price Paid: $_____
Date Purchased: _____
Tag Generation: _____

Daisy™

34

Cow · #4006
Issued: June 25, 1994
Retired: September 15, 1998

Market Value:
⑤- $12
④- $16
③- $110
②- $230
①- $340

Daisy drinks milk each night
So her coat is shiny and bright
Milk is good for your hair and skin
What a way for your day to begin!

Birthdate: May 10, 1994
Price Paid: $_____
Date Purchased: _____
Tag Generation: _____

COLLECTOR'S
VALUE GUIDE™

Value
Totals _____

35

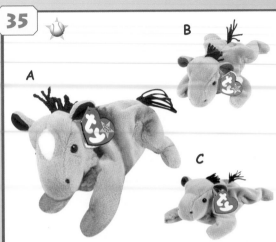

Derby™

Horse · #4008
Issued: June 3, 1995
Current – Easy To Find

Market Value:
A. Star (Dec. 97-Current)
⑤- $_____
B. Coarse Mane
(Est. Late 95–Dec. 97)
④- $35
③- $700
C. Fine Mane
(Est. June 95–Late 95)
③- $3,900

Birthdate: September 16, 1995
Price Paid: $_____
Date Purchased: _____
Tag Generation: _____

All the other horses used to tattle
Because Derby never wore his saddle
He left the stables, and the horses too
Just so Derby can be with you!

36

B

Digger™

Crab · #4027
Issued: June 25, 1994
Retired: May 11, 1997

Market Value:
A. Red (June 95-May 97)
④- $145
③- $330
B. Orange (June 94-June 95)
③- $825
②- $900
①- $975

A

Birthdate: August 23, 1995
Price Paid: $_____
Date Purchased: _____
Tag Generation: _____

Digging in the sand and walking sideways
That's how Digger spends her days
Hard on the outside but sweet deep inside
Basking in the sun and riding the tide!

Value
Totals _____

COLLECTOR'S
VALUE GUIDE™

37

Doby™

Doberman · #4110
Issued: January 1, 1997
Current - Easy To Find

Market Value:
5 - $_____
4 - $13

This dog is little but he has might
Keep him close when you sleep at night
He lays around with nothing to do
Until he sees it's time to protect you!

Birthdate: October 9, 1996
Price Paid: $_____
Date Purchased: _____
Tag Generation: _____

38

Doodle™

(name changed from "Strut™")

Rooster · #4171
Issued: May 11, 1997
Retired: 1997

Market Value:
4 - $50

Listen closely to "cock-a-doodle-doo"
What's the rooster saying to you?
Hurry, wake up sleepy head
We have lots to do, get out of bed!

Birthdate: March 8, 1996
Price Paid: $_____
Date Purchased: _____
Tag Generation: _____

COLLECTOR'S
VALUE GUIDE™

Value
Totals _____

39

Dotty™

Dalmatian · #4100
Issued: May 11, 1997
Current – Easy To Find

Market Value:
⑤- $_____
④- $15

Birthdate: October 17, 1996
Price Paid: $_____
Date Purchased: _____
Tag Generation: _____

The Beanies all thought it was a big joke
While writing her tag, their ink pen broke
She got in the way, and got all spotty
So now the Beanies call her Dotty!

40

Early™

Robin · #4190
Issued: May 30, 1998
Current – Moderate To Find

Market Value:
⑤- $_____

Birthdate: February 20, 1997
or March 20, 1997
Price Paid: $_____
Date Purchased: _____
Tag Generation: _____

Early is a red breasted robin
For a worm he'll soon be bobbin'
Always known as a sign of spring
This happy robin loves to sing!

Value
Totals _____

COLLECTOR'S
VALUE GUIDE™

41

Ears™

Rabbit · #4018
Issued: January 7, 1996
Retired: May 1, 1998

Market Value:
⑤-$23
④-$28
③-$115

He's been eating carrots so long
Didn't understand what was wrong
   Couldn't see the board during classes
    Until the doctor gave him glasses!

Birthdate: April 18, 1995
Price Paid: $_____
Date Purchased: _____
Tag Generation: _____

42

Echo™

Dolphin · #4180
Issued: May 11, 1997
Retired: May 1, 1998

Market Value:
⑤-$22
④-$28

Echo the dolphin lives in the sea
Playing with her friends, like you and me
Through the waves she echoes the sound
"I'm so glad to have you around!"

Birthdate: December 21, 1996
Price Paid: $_____
Date Purchased: _____
Tag Generation: _____

Value
Totals _____

43

Erin™

Bear • #4186
Issued: January 31, 1998
Current – Very Hard To Find

Market Value:
💲- $_____

Birthdate: March 17, 1997
Price Paid: $_____
Date Purchased: _____
Tag Generation: _____

Named after the beautiful Emerald Isle
This Beanie Baby will make you smile,
A bit of luck, a pot of gold,
Light up the faces, both young and old!

44

Fetch™

Golden Retriever • #4189
Issued: May 30, 1998
Current – Moderate To Find

Market Value:
💲- $_____

Birthdate: February 4, 1997
Price Paid: $_____
Date Purchased: _____
Tag Generation: _____

Fetch is alert at the crack of dawn
Walking through dew drops on the lawn
Always golden, loyal and true
This little puppy is the one for you!

Value
Totals _____

COLLECTOR'S
VALUE GUIDE™

45

Flash™

Dolphin · #4021
Issued: January 8, 1994
Retired: May 11, 1997

Market Value:
④- $135
③- $220
②- $380
①- $450

You know dolphins are a smart breed
Our friend Flash knows how to read
Splash the whale is the one who taught her
Although reading is difficult under the water!

Birthdate: May 13, 1993
Price Paid: $_____
Date Purchased: _____
Tag Generation: _____

46

Fleece™

Lamb · #4125
Issued: January 1, 1997
Current – Easy To Find

Market Value:
⑤- $_____
④- $13

Fleece would like to sing a lullaby
But please be patient, she's rather shy
When you sleep, keep her by your ear
Her song will leave you nothing to fear.

Birthdate: March 21, 1996
Price Paid: $_____
Date Purchased: _____
Tag Generation: _____

47

Flip™

Cat · #4012
Issued: January 7, 1996
Retired: October 1, 1997

Market Value:
4- $42
3- $150

Birthdate: February 28, 1995
Price Paid: $_____
Date Purchased: _____
Tag Generation: _____

Flip the cat is an acrobat
She loves playing on her mat
This cat flips with such grace and flair
She can somersault in mid air!

48

Floppity™

Bunny · #4118
Issued: January 1, 1997
Retired: May 1, 1998

Market Value:
5- $26
4- $32

Birthdate: May 28, 1996
Price Paid: $_____
Date Purchased: _____
Tag Generation: _____

Floppity hops from here to there
Searching for eggs without a care
Lavender coat from head to toe
All dressed up and nowhere to go!

Value
Totals _____

COLLECTOR'S
VALUE GUIDE™

Flutter™

Butterfly · #4043
Issued: June 3, 1995
Retired: June 15, 1996

Market Value:
❸- $1,125

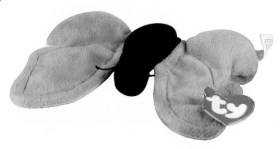

No Poem_____
_____
_____
_____

Birthdate: N/A
Price Paid: $_____
Date Purchased: _____
Tag Generation: _____

Fortune™

Panda · #4196
Issued: May 30, 1998
Current – Hard To Find

Market Value:
❺- $_____

Nibbling on a bamboo tree
This little panda is hard to see
You're so lucky with this one you found
Only a few are still around!

Birthdate: December 6, 1997
Price Paid: $_____
Date Purchased: _____
Tag Generation: _____

Value
Totals _____

51

Freckles™

Leopard · #4066
Issued: June 15, 1996
Current – Easy To Find

Market Value:
⑤- $_____
④- $13

Birthdate: June 3, 1996
or July 28, 1996
Price Paid: $_____
Date Purchased: _____
Tag Generation: _____

From the trees he hunts prey
In the night and in the day
He's the king of camouflage
Look real close, he's no mirage!

52

Garcia™

Bear · #4051
Issued: January 7, 1996
Retired: May 11, 1997

Market Value:
④- $200
③- $290

Birthdate: August 1, 1995
Price Paid: $_____
Date Purchased: _____
Tag Generation: _____

The Beanies use to follow him around
Because Garcia traveled from town to town
He's pretty popular as you can see
Some even say he's legendary!

Value
Totals _____

COLLECTOR'S
VALUE GUIDE™

53

Gigi™

Poodle · #4191
Issued: May 30, 1998
Current – Moderate To Find

Market Value:
⑤- $_____

Prancing and dancing all down the street
Thinking her hairdo is oh so neat
Always so careful in the wind and rain
She's a dog that is anything but plain!

Birthdate: April 7, 1997
Price Paid: $_____
Date Purchased: _____
Tag Generation: _____

54

Glory™

Bear · #4188
Issued: May 30, 1998
Current – Very Hard To Find

Market Value:
⑤- $_____

Wearing the flag for all to see
Symbol of freedom for you and me
Red white and blue – Independence Day
Happy Birthday USA!

Birthdate: July 4, 1997
Price Paid: $_____
Date Purchased: _____
Tag Generation: _____

55

Gobbles™

Turkey · #4034
Issued: October 1, 1997
Current – Moderate To Find

Market Value:
5 – $_____
4 – $25

Birthdate: November 27, 1996
Price Paid: $_____
Date Purchased: _____
Tag Generation: _____

Gobbles the turkey loves to eat
Once a year she has a feast
I have a secret I'd like to divulge
If she eats too much her tummy will bulge!

56

Goldie™

Goldfish · #4023
Issued: June 25, 1994
Retired: December 31, 1997

Market Value:
5 – $53
4 – $53
3 – $140
2 – $260
1 – $390

Birthdate: November 14, 1994
Price Paid: $_____
Date Purchased: _____
Tag Generation: _____

She's got rhythm, she's got soul
What more to like in a fish bowl?
Through sound waves Goldie swam
Because this goldfish likes to jam!

Value
Totals _____

COLLECTOR'S
VALUE GUIDE™

Gracie™

Swan · #4126
Issued: January 1, 1997
Retired: May 1, 1998

Market Value:
- ⑤ – $22
- ④ – $28

As a duckling, she was confused,
Birds on the lake were quite amused.
Poking fun until she would cry,
Now the most beautiful swan at Ty!

Birthdate: June 17, 1996
Price Paid: $_____
Date Purchased: _____
Tag Generation: _____

Grunt™

Razorback · #4092
Issued: January 7, 1996
Retired: May 11, 1997

Market Value:
- ④ – $190
- ③ – $290

Some Beanies think Grunt is tough
No surprise, he's scary enough
But if you take him home you'll see
Grunt is the sweetest Beanie Baby!

Birthdate: July 19, 1995
Price Paid: $_____
Date Purchased: _____
Tag Generation: _____

Value
Totals _____

59

NEW!

Halo™

Angel · #4208
Issued: September 30, 1998
Current – Just Released

Market Value:
⑤- $_____

Birthdate: August 31, 1998
Price Paid: $_____
Date Purchased: _____
Tag Generation: _____

When you sleep, I'm always here
Don't be afraid, I am near
Watching over you with lots of love
Your guardian angel from above!

60

B

A

Happy™

Hippo · #4061
Issued: June 25, 1994
Retired: May 1, 1998

Market Value:
A. Lavender (June 95–May 98)
⑤- $30
④- $34
③- $325
B. Gray (June 94–June 95)
③- $800
②- $850
①- $950

Birthdate: February 25, 1994
Price Paid: $_____
Date Purchased: _____
Tag Generation: _____

Happy the Hippo loves to wade
In the river and in the shade
When Happy shoots water out of his snout
You know he's happy without a doubt!

Value
Totals _____

COLLECTOR'S
VALUE GUIDE™

61

Hippity™

Bunny · #4119
Issued: January 1, 1997
Retired: May 1, 1998

Market Value:
♥5- $26
♥4- $32

Hippity is a cute little bunny
  Dressed in green, he looks quite funny
  Twitching his nose in the air
  Sniffing a flower here and there!

Birthdate: June 1, 1996
Price Paid: $_____
Date Purchased: _____
Tag Generation: _____

62

Hissy™

Snake · #4185
Issued: December 31, 1997
Current - Easy To Find

Market Value:
♥5- $_____

Curled and coiled and ready to play
  He waits for you patiently every day
  He'll keep his best friend, but not his skin
And stay with you through thick and thin.

Birthdate: April 4, 1997
Price Paid: $_____
Date Purchased: _____
Tag Generation: _____

63

Hoot™

Owl • #4073
Issued: January 7, 1996
Retired: October 1, 1997

Market Value:
④-$52
③-$130

Birthdate: August 9, 1995
Price Paid: $_____
Date Purchased: _____
Tag Generation: _____

Late to bed, late to rise
Nevertheless, Hoot's quite wise
Studies by candlelight, nothing new
Like a president, do you know Whooo?

64

Hoppity™

Bunny • #4117
Issued: January 1, 1997
Retired: May 1, 1998

Market Value:
⑤-$26
④-$32

Birthdate: April 3, 1996
Price Paid: $_____
Date Purchased: _____
Tag Generation: _____

Hopscotch is what she likes to play
If you don't join in, she'll hop away
So play a game if you have the time,
She likes to play, rain or shine!

Value
Totals _____

COLLECTOR'S
VALUE GUIDE™

65

Humphrey™

Camel · #4060
Issued: June 25, 1994
Retired: June 15, 1995

Market Value:
❸ – $2,000
❷ – $2,150
❶ – $2,450

Birthdate: N/A

No Poem_____
_____
_____
_____

Price Paid: $_____
Date Purchased: _____
Tag Generation: _____

66

Iggy™
(commonly mistagged
as "Rainbow™")

Iguana · #4038
Issued: December 31, 1997
Current – Moderate To Find

Market Value:
❺ – $_____

Birthdate: August 12, 1997

Sitting on a rock, basking in the sun
Is this iguana's idea of fun
Towel and glasses, book and beach chair
His life is so perfect without a care!

Price Paid: $_____
Date Purchased: _____
Tag Generation: _____

COLLECTOR'S
VALUE GUIDE™

Value
Totals _____

67

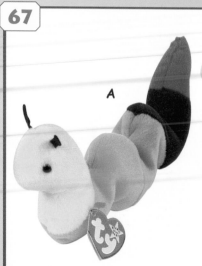

Inch™

Inchworm · #4044
Issued: June 3, 1995
Retired: May 1, 1998

Market Value:
A. Yarn Antennas
   (Est. Mid 96-May 98)
   ⑤- $25
   ④- $35
B. Felt Antennas
   (Est. June 95-Mid 96)
   ④- $185
   ③- $200

Birthdate: September 3, 1995
Price Paid: $_____
Date Purchased: _____
Tag Generation: _____

Inch the worm is a friend of mine
He goes so slow all the time
Inching around from here to there
Traveling the world without a care!

68

Inky™

Octopus · #4028
Issued: June 25, 1994
Retired: May 1, 1998

Market Value:
A. Pink (June 95-May 98)
   ⑤- $38 ④- $45 ③- $310
B. Tan With Mouth
   (Sept. 94-June 95)
   ③- $730 ②- $775
C. Tan Without Mouth
   (June 94-Sept. 94)
   ②- $850 ①- $900

Birthdate: November 29, 1994
Price Paid: $_____
Date Purchased: _____
Tag Generation: _____

Inky's head is big and round
As he swims he makes no sound
If you need a hand, don't hesitate
Inky can help because he has eight!

Value
Totals _____

69

Jabber™

Parrot • #4197
Issued: May 30, 1998
Current – Moderate To Find

Market Value:
♥- $_____

Teaching Jabber to move his beak
A large vocabulary he now can speak
Jabber will repeat what you say
Teach him a new word everyday!

Birthdate: October 10, 1997
Price Paid: $_____
Date Purchased: _____
Tag Generation: _____

70

Jake™

Mallard Duck • #4199
Issued: May 30, 1998
Current – Moderate To Find

Market Value:
♥- $_____

Jake the drake likes to splash in a puddle
Take him home and give him a cuddle
Quack, Quack, Quack, he will say
He's so glad you're here to play!

Birthdate: April 16, 1997
Price Paid: $_____
Date Purchased: _____
Tag Generation: _____

COLLECTOR'S
VALUE GUIDE™

Value
Totals _____

71

Jolly™

Walrus · #4082
Issued: May 11, 1997
Retired: May 1, 1998

Market Value:
⑤ – $25
④ – $30

Birthdate: December 2, 1996
Price Paid: $_____
Date Purchased: _____
Tag Generation: _____

Jolly the walrus is not very serious
He laughs and laughs until he's delirious
He often reminds me of my dad
Always happy, never sad!

72

Kiwi™

Toucan · #4070
Issued: June 3, 1995
Retired: January 1, 1997

Market Value:
④ – $195
③ – $280

Birthdate: September 16, 1995
Price Paid: $_____
Date Purchased: _____
Tag Generation: _____

Kiwi waits for the April showers
Watching a garden bloom with flowers
There trees grow with fruit that's sweet
I'm sure you'll guess his favorite treat!

Value
Totals _____

COLLECTOR'S
VALUE GUIDE™

73

Kuku™

Cockatoo · #4192
Issued: May 30, 1998
Current – Moderate To Find

Market Value:
5-$_____

Birthdate: January 5, 1997
Price Paid: $_____
Date Purchased: _____
Tag Generation: _____

This fancy bird loves to converse
He talks in poems, rhythms and verse
So take him home and give him some time
You'll be surprised how he can rhyme!

74

Lefty™

Donkey · #4085
Issued: June 15, 1996
Retired: January 1, 1997

Market Value:
4-$330

Birthdate: July 4, 1996
Price Paid: $_____
Date Purchased: _____
Tag Generation: _____

Donkeys to the left, elephants to the right
Often seems like a crazy sight
This whole game seems very funny
Until you realize they're spending
Your money!

COLLECTOR'S
VALUE GUIDE™

Value
Totals _____

75

Legs™

Frog · #4020
Issued: January 8, 1994
Retired: October 1, 1997

Market Value:
- ❹ - $32
- ❸ - $125
- ❷ - $275
- ❶ - $350

Birthdate: April 25, 1993
Price Paid: $_____
Date Purchased: _____
Tag Generation: _____

Legs lives in a hollow log
Legs likes to play leap frog
If you like to hang out at the lake
Legs will be the new friend you'll make!

76

Libearty™

Bear · #4057
Issued: June 15, 1996
Retired: January 1, 1997

Market Value:
- ❹ - $400

Birthdate: Summer 1996
Price Paid: $_____
Date Purchased: _____
Tag Generation: _____

I am called libearty
I wear the flag for all to see
Hope and freedom is my way
That's why I wear flag USA

Value
Totals _____

COLLECTOR'S
VALUE GUIDE™

Lizzy™

Lizard · #4033
Issued: June 3, 1995
Retired: December 31, 1997

Market Value:
A. Blue (Jan. 96-Dec. 97)
⑤- $32
④- $32
③- $360
B. Tie-dye (June 95–Jan. 96)
③- $1,100

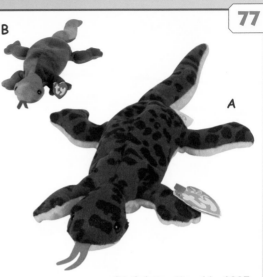

A

B

Lizzy loves Legs the frog
She hides with him under logs
Both of them search for flies
Underneath the clear blue skies!

Birthdate: May 11, 1995
Price Paid: $_____
Date Purchased: _____
Tag Generation: _____

NEW!

Loosy™

Goose · #4206
Issued: September 30, 1998
Current – Just Released

Market Value:
⑤- $_____

A tale has been told
Of a goose that laid gold
But try as she might
Loosy's eggs are just white!

Birthdate: March 29, 1998
Price Paid: $_____
Date Purchased: _____
Tag Generation: _____

Value
Totals _____

78

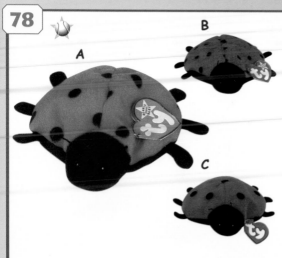

Lucky™

Ladybug · #4040
Issued: June 25, 1994
Retired: May 1, 1998

Market Value:
A. Approx. 11 Printed Spots
(Feb. 96–May 98)
⑤-$28 ④-$35
B. Approx. 21 Printed Spots
(Est. Mid 96–Late 96)
④-$625
C. Approx. 7 Felt Glued-On
Spots (June 94–Feb. 96)
③-$225 ②-$350
①-$425

Birthdate: May 1, 1995
Price Paid: $_____
Date Purchased: _____
Tag Generation: _____

Lucky the lady bug loves the lotto
"Someone must win" that's her motto
But save your dimes and even a penny
Don't spend on the lotto and
You'll have many!

80

Magic™

Dragon · #4088
Issued: June 3, 1995
Retired: December 31, 1997

Market Value:
A. Pale Pink Thread
(June 95–Dec. 97)
④-$55
③-$145
B. Hot Pink Thread
(Est. Mid 96–Early 97)
④-$80

Birthdate: September 5, 1995
Price Paid: $_____
Date Purchased: _____
Tag Generation: _____

Magic the dragon lives in a dream
The most beautiful that you have ever seen
Through magic lands she likes to fly
Look up and watch her, way up high!

Value
Totals _____

COLLECTOR'S
VALUE GUIDE™

81

Manny™

Manatee · #4081
Issued: January 7, 1996
Retired: May 11, 1997

Market Value:
④- $190
③- $250

Manny is sometimes called a sea cow
She likes to twirl and likes to bow
Manny sure is glad you bought her
Because it's so lonely under water!

Birthdate: June 8, 1995
Price Paid: $_____
Date Purchased: _____
Tag Generation: _____

82

Maple™
(exclusive to Canada)

Bear · #4600
Issued: January 1, 1997
Current – Impossible To Find

Market Value
(in U.S. market):
A. "Maple™" Tush Tag
   (Est. Early 97-Current)
   ⑤- $295
   ④- $310
B. "Pride™" Tush Tag
   (Est. Early 97)
   ④- $670

B
The Beanie Babies Collection™
ty
Pride
HAND MADE IN CHINA
© 1996 TY INC.
OAKBROOK IL U.S.A.
SURFACE WASHABLE
ALL NEW MATERIAL
POLYESTER FIBER
& PVC PELLETS CE
REG. NO. PA. 1965(KR)

A

Maple the bear likes to ski
With his friends, he plays hockey.
He loves his pancakes and eats every crumb
Can you guess which country he's from?

Birthdate: July 1, 1996
Price Paid: $_____
Date Purchased: _____
Tag Generation: _____

COLLECTOR'S
VALUE GUIDE™

Value
Totals _____

83

Mel™

Koala · #4162
Issued: January 1, 1997
Current – Easy To Find

Market Value:
⑤- $_____
④- $13

Birthdate: January 15, 1996
Price Paid: $_____
Date Purchased: _____
Tag Generation: _____

How do you name a Koala bear?
It's rather tough, I do declare!
It confuses me, I get into a funk
I'll name him Mel, after my favorite hunk!

84

B

Mystic™

Unicorn · #4007
Issued: June 25, 1994
Current – Moderate To Find

Market Value:
A. Iridescent Horn
(Oct. 97-Current)
⑤- $_____ ④- $30
B. Brown Horn/Coarse Mane
(Est. Late 95–Oct. 97)
④- $45 ③- $120
C. Brown Horn/Fine Mane
(Est. June 94–Late 95)
③- $295 ②- $400 ①- $525

A

C

Birthdate: May 21, 1994
Price Paid: $_____
Date Purchased: _____
Tag Generation: _____

Once upon a time so far away
A unicorn was born one day in May
Keep Mystic with you, she's a prize
You'll see the magic in her blue eyes!

Value
Totals _____

COLLECTOR'S
VALUE GUIDE™

85

Nana™
(name changed to "Bongo™")

Monkey · #4067
Issued: June 3, 1995
Retired: 1995

Market Value:
- $4,100

No Poem_____
_____
_____
_____

Birthdate: N/A
Price Paid: $_____
Date Purchased: _____
Tag Generation: _____

86

Nanook™

Husky · #4104
Issued: May 11, 1997
Current – Moderate To Find

Market Value:
⑤- $_____
④- $16

Nanook is a dog that loves cold weather
To him a sled is light as a feather
Over the snow and through the slush
He runs at hearing the cry of "mush"!

Birthdate: November 21, 1996
Price Paid: $_____
Date Purchased: _____
Tag Generation: _____

COLLECTOR'S
VALUE GUIDE™

Value
Totals _____

87

B

A

C

Nip™

Cat · #4003
Issued: January 7, 1995
Retired: December 31, 1997

Market Value:
**A. White Paws
(Feb. 96-Dec. 97)**
⑤-$34 ④-$34 ③-$340
**B. All Gold
(Jan. 96–March 96)**
③-$950
**C. White Face
(Jan. 95–Jan. 96)**
③-$525 ②-$560

Birthdate: March 6, 1994
Price Paid: $_____
Date Purchased: _____
Tag Generation: _____

His name is Nipper, but we call him Nip
His best friend is a black cat named Zip
Nip likes to run in races for fun
He runs so fast he's always number one!

88

Nuts™

Squirrel · #4114
Issued: January 1, 1997
Current – Easy To Find

Market Value:
⑤-$_____
④-$13

Birthdate: January 21, 1996
Price Paid: $_____
Date Purchased: _____
Tag Generation: _____

With his bushy tail, he'll scamper up a tree
The most cheerful critter you'll ever see,
He's nuts about nuts, and he loves to chat
Have you ever seen a squirrel like that?

Value
Totals _____

COLLECTOR'S
VALUE GUIDE™

Patti™

Platypus · #4025
Issued: January 8, 1994
Retired: May 1, 1998

Market Value:
A. Magenta (Feb. 95-May 98)
⑤- $28
④- $35
③- $275
B. Maroon (Jan. 94-Feb. 95)
③- $850
②- $1,000
①- $1,100

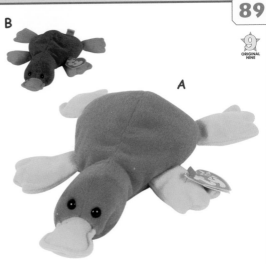

9
ORIGINAL
NINE

Ran into Patti one day while walking
Believe me she wouldn't stop talking
Listened and listened to her speak
That would explain her extra large beak!

Birthdate: January 6, 1993
Price Paid: $_____
Date Purchased: _____
Tag Generation: _____

Peace™

Bear · #4053
Issued: May 11, 1997
Current – Very Hard To Find

Market Value:
⑤- $_____
④- $40

All races, all colors, under the sun
Join hands together and have some fun
Dance to the music, rock and roll is the sound
Symbols of peace and love abound!

Birthdate: February 1, 1996
Price Paid: $_____
Date Purchased: _____
Tag Generation: _____

COLLECTOR'S
VALUE GUIDE™

Value
Totals _____

91

Peanut™

Elephant · #4062
Issued: June 3, 1995
Retired: May 1, 1998

Market Value:
A. Light Blue
(Oct. 95-May 98)
⑤- $25
④- $30
③- $1,200
B. Dark Blue
(June 95–Oct. 95)
③- $5,300

Birthdate: January 25, 1995
Price Paid: $_____
Date Purchased: _____
Tag Generation: _____

Peanut the elephant walks on tip-toes
Quietly sneaking wherever she goes
She'll sneak up on you and a hug
You will get
Peanut is a friend you won't soon forget!

92

Peking™

Panda · #4013
Issued: June 25, 1994
Retired: January 7, 1996

Market Value:
③- $2,200
②- $2,350
①- $2,400

Birthdate: N/A
Price Paid: $_____
Date Purchased: _____
Tag Generation: _____

No Poem_____
_____
_____

Value
Totals _____

COLLECTOR'S
VALUE GUIDE™

93

Pinchers™

Lobster · #4026
Issued: January 8, 1994
Retired: May 1, 1998

Market Value:
A. "Pinchers™" Swing Tag
(Jan. 94-May 98)
⑤- $26
④- $30
③- $110
②- $230
①- $340
B. "Punchers™" Swing Tag
(Est. Early 94)
①- $3,950

B

The Beanie Babies Collection
Punchers™ style 4026
© 1993 Ty Inc. Oakbrook, IL. USA
All Rights Reserved. Caution:
Remove this tag before giving
toy to a child. For ages 5 and up.
Handmade in Korea.
Surface
Wash.

A

9
ORIGINAL
NINE

This lobster loves to pinch
Eating his food inch by inch
Balancing carefully with his tail
Moving forward slow as a snail!

Birthdate: June 19, 1993
Price Paid: $_____
Date Purchased: _____
Tag Generation: _____

94

Pinky™

Flamingo · #4072
Issued: June 3, 1995
Current – Easy To Find

Market Value:
⑤- $_____
④- $14
③- $135

Pinky loves the everglades
From the hottest pink she's made
With floppy legs and big orange beak
She's the Beanie that you seek!

Birthdate: February 13, 1995
Price Paid: $_____
Date Purchased: _____
Tag Generation: _____

95

Pouch™

Kangaroo · #4161
Issued: January 1, 1997
Current – Easy To Find

Market Value:
⑤- $_____
④- $14

Birthdate: November 6, 1996
Price Paid: $_____
Date Purchased: _____
Tag Generation: _____

My little pouch is handy I've found
It helps me carry my baby around
I hop up and down without any fear
Knowing my baby is safe and near.

96

Pounce™

Cat · #4122
Issued: December 31, 1997
Current – Easy To Find

Market Value:
⑤- $_____

Birthdate: August 28, 1997
Price Paid: $_____
Date Purchased: _____
Tag Generation: _____

Sneaking and slinking down the hall
To pounce upon a fluffy yarn ball
Under the tables, around the chairs
Through the rooms and down the stairs!

Value
Totals _____

COLLECTOR'S
VALUE GUIDE™

97

Prance™

Cat • #4123
Issued: December 31, 1997
Current – Easy To Find

Market Value:
⑤- $_____

She darts around and swats the air
Then looks confused when nothing's there
Pick her up and pet her soft fur
Listen closely, and you'll hear her purr!

Birthdate: November 20, 1997
Price Paid: $_____
Date Purchased: _____
Tag Generation: _____

98

Princess™   B

Bear • #4300
Issued: October 29, 1997
Current – Very Hard To Find

Market Value:
A. "P.E. Pellets" On Tush Tag
   (Est. Late 97-Current)
   ④- $_____
B. "P.V.C. Pellets" On Tush
   Tag (Est. Late 97)
   ④- $150

A

Like an angel, she came from heaven above
She shared her compassion, her pain, her love
She only stayed with us long enough to teach
The world to share, to give, to reach.

Birthdate: N/A
Price Paid: $_____
Date Purchased: _____
Tag Generation: _____

99

Puffer™

Puffin · #4181
Issued: December 31, 1997
Retired: September 18, 1998

Market Value:
⑤ – $12

Birthdate: November 3, 1997
Price Paid: $_____
Date Purchased: _____
Tag Generation: _____

What in the world does a puffin do?
We're sure that you would like to know too
We asked Puffer how she spends her days
Before she answered, she flew away!

100

Pugsly™

Pug Dog · #4106
Issued: May 11, 1997
Current – Easy To Find

Market Value:
⑤ – $_____
④ – $15

Birthdate: May 2, 1996
Price Paid: $_____
Date Purchased: _____
Tag Generation: _____

Pugsly is picky about what he will wear
Never a spot, a stain or a tear
Image is something of which he'll gloat
Until he noticed his wrinkled coat!

Value
Totals _____

COLLECTOR'S
VALUE GUIDE™

Pumkin'™

Pumpkin · #4205
Issued: September 30, 1998
Current – Just Released

Market Value:
⑤- $_____

Ghost and goblins are out tonight
Witches try hard to cause fright
This little pumpkin is very sweet
He only wants to trick or treat!

Birthdate: October 31, 1998
Price Paid: $_____
Date Purchased: _____
Tag Generation: _____

Quackers™

B

Duck · #4024
Issued: June 25, 1994
Retired: May 1, 1998

Market Value:
A. "Quackers™" With Wings
  (Jan. 95-May 98)
    ⑤- $25 ④- $27
    ③- $125 ②- $800
B. "Quacker™" Without
  Wings (June 94–Jan. 95)
    ②- $2,200 ①- $2,300

A

There is a duck by the name of Quackers
Every night he eats animal crackers
He swims in a lake that's clear and blue
But he'll come to the shore to be with you!

Birthdate: April 19, 1994
Price Paid: $_____
Date Purchased: _____
Tag Generation: _____

Value
Totals _____

103

Radar™

Bat · #4091
Issued: September 1, 1995
Retired: May 11, 1997

Market Value:
❹ - $190
❸ - $265

Birthdate: October 30, 1995
Price Paid: $_____
Date Purchased: _____
Tag Generation: _____

Radar the bat flies late at night
He can soar to an amazing height
If you see something as high as a star
Take a good look, it might be Radar!

104

B

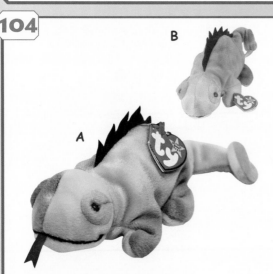

A

Rainbow™

(commonly mistagged
as "Iggy™")

Chameleon · #4037
Issued: December 31, 1997
Current – Moderate To Find

Market Value:
A. Tongue (June 98-Current)
❺ - $_____
B. No Tongue
(Dec. 97-June 98)
❺ - $17

Birthdate: October 14, 1997
Price Paid: $_____
Date Purchased: _____
Tag Generation: _____

Red, green, blue and yellow
This chameleon is a colorful fellow.
A blend of colors, his own unique hue
Rainbow was made especially for you!

Value
Totals _____

COLLECTOR'S
VALUE GUIDE™

105

Rex™

Tyrannosaurus · #4086
Issued: June 3, 1995
Retired: June 15, 1996

Market Value:
③-$950

No Poem_____
_____
_____
_____

Birthdate: N/A
Price Paid: $_____
Date Purchased: _____
Tag Generation: _____

106

Righty™

Elephant · #4086
Issued: June 15, 1996
Retired: January 1, 1997

Market Value:
④-$330

Donkeys to the left, elephants to the right
Often seems like a crazy sight
This whole game seems very funny
Until you realize they're spending
Your money!

Birthdate: July 4, 1996
Price Paid: $_____
Date Purchased: _____
Tag Generation: _____

COLLECTOR'S
VALUE GUIDE™

Value
Totals _____

107

Ringo™

Raccoon • #4014
Issued: January 7, 1996
Retired: September 16, 1998

Market Value:

⑤- $12
④- $15
③- $100

Birthdate: July 14, 1995
Price Paid: $_____
Date Purchased: _____
Tag Generation: _____

Ringo hides behind his mask
He will come out, if you should ask
He loves to chitter. He loves to chatter
Just about anything, it doesn't matter!

108

NEW!

Roam™

Buffalo • #4209
Issued: September 30, 1998
Current – Just Released

Market Value:
⑤- $_____

Birthdate: September 27, 1998
Price Paid: $_____
Date Purchased: _____
Tag Generation: _____

Once roaming wild on American land
Tall and strong, wooly and grand
So rare and special is this guy
Find him quickly, he's quite a buy!

Value
Totals _____

COLLECTOR'S
VALUE GUIDE™

Roary™

109

Lion · #4069
Issued: May 11, 1997
Current - Easy To Find

Market Value:
⑤- $_____
④- $14

Deep in the jungle they crowned him king
But being brave is not his thing
A cowardly lion some may say
He hears his roar and runs away!

Birthdate: February 20, 1996
Price Paid: $_____
Date Purchased: _____
Tag Generation: _____

Rocket™

110

Blue Jay · #4202
Issued: May 30, 1998
Current – Moderate To Find

Market Value:
⑤- $_____

Rocket is the fastest blue jay ever
He flies in all sorts of weather
Aerial tricks are his specialty
He's so entertaining for you and me!

Birthdate: March 12, 1997
Price Paid: $_____
Date Purchased: _____
Tag Generation: _____

111

Rover™

Dog • #4101
Issued: June 15, 1996
Retired: May 1, 1998

Market Value:
5 – $25
4 – $30

Birthdate: May 30, 1996
Price Paid: $_____
Date Purchased: _____
Tag Generation: _____

This dog is red and his name is Rover
If you call him he is sure to come over
He barks and plays with all his might
But worry not, he won't bite!

112

NEW!

Santa™

Elf • #4203
Issued: September 30, 1998
Current – Just Released

Market Value:
5 – $_____

Birthdate: December 6, 1998
Price Paid: $_____
Date Purchased: _____
Tag Generation: _____

Known by all in his suit of red
Piles of presents on his sled
Generous and giving, he brings us joy
Peace and love, plus this special toy!

Value
Totals _____

COLLECTOR'S
VALUE GUIDE™

113

Scoop™

Pelican · #4107
Issued: June 15, 1996
Current – Easy To Find

Market Value:
- ⑤ - $_____
- ④ - $14

All day long he scoops up fish
To fill his bill, is his wish
Diving fast and diving low
Hoping those fish are very slow!

Birthdate: July 1, 1996
Price Paid: $_____
Date Purchased: _____
Tag Generation: _____

114

NEW!

Scorch™

Dragon · #4210
Issued: September 30, 1998
Current – Just Released

Market Value:
- ⑤ - $_____

A magical mystery with glowing wings
Made by wizards and other things
Known to breathe fire with lots of smoke
Scorch is really a friendly ol' bloke!

Birthdate: July 31, 1998
Price Paid: $_____
Date Purchased: _____
Tag Generation: _____

115

Scottie™

Scottish Terrier • #4102
Issued: June 15, 1996
Retired: May 1, 1998

Market Value:
⑤-$32
④-$38

Birthdate: June 3, 1996
or June 15, 1996
Price Paid: $_____
Date Purchased: _____
Tag Generation: _____

Scottie is a friendly sort
Even though his legs are short
He is always happy as can be
His best friends are you and me!

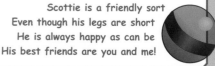

116

Seamore™

Seal • #4029
Issued: June 25, 1994
Retired: October 1, 1997

Market Value:
④-$180
③-$250
②-$380
①-$500

Birthdate: December 14, 1996
Price Paid: $_____
Date Purchased: _____
Tag Generation: _____

Seamore is a little white seal
Fish and clams are her favorite meal
Playing and laughing in the sand
She's the happiest seal in the land!

Value
Totals _____

COLLECTOR'S
VALUE GUIDE™

Seaweed™

Otter · #4080
Issued: January 7, 1996
Retired: September 19, 1998

Market Value:
- ⑤- $22
- ④- $25
- ③- $100

Seaweed is what she likes to eat
It's supposed to be a delicious treat
Have you tried a treat from the water
If you haven't, maybe you "otter"!

Birthdate: March 19, 1996
Price Paid: $_____
Date Purchased: _____
Tag Generation: _____

Slither™

Snake · #4031
Issued: June 25, 1994
Retired: June 15, 1995

Market Value:
- ③- $2,050
- ②- $2,100
- ①- $2,300

No Poem_____
_____
_____
_____

Birthdate: N/A
Price Paid: $_____
Date Purchased: _____
Tag Generation: _____

Value
Totals _____

119

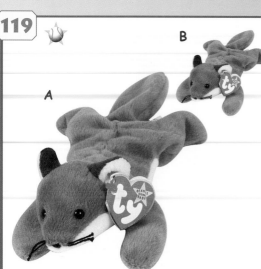

B

A

Sly™

Fox · #4115
Issued: June 15, 1996
Retired: September 22, 1998

Market Value:
A. White Belly
(Aug. 96-Sept. 98)
⑤- $12
④- $15
B. Brown Belly
(June 96-Aug. 96)
④- $185

Birthdate: September 12, 1996
Price Paid: $_____
Date Purchased: _____
Tag Generation: _____

Sly is a fox and tricky is he
Please don't chase him, let him be
If you want him, just say when
He'll peek out from his den!

120

Smoochy™

Frog · #4039
Issued: December 31, 1997
Current – Easy To Find

Market Value:
⑤- $_____

Birthdate: October 1, 1997
Price Paid: $_____
Date Purchased: _____
Tag Generation: _____

Is he a frog or maybe a prince?
This confusion makes him wince
Find the answer, help him with this
Be the one to give him a kiss!

Value
Totals _____

COLLECTOR'S
VALUE GUIDE™

121

Snip™

Siamese Cat · #4120
Issued: January 1, 1997
Current – Easy To Find

Market Value:
5 - $_____
4 - $14

Snip the cat is Siamese
She'll be your friend if you please
So toss her a toy or a piece of string
   Playing with you is her favorite thing!

Birthdate: October 22, 1996
Price Paid: $_____
Date Purchased: _____
Tag Generation: _____

122

Snort™

Bull · #4002
Issued: January 1, 1997
Retired: September 15, 1998

Market Value:
5 - $12
4 - $14

Although Snort is not so tall
He loves to play basketball
He is a star player in his dreams
Can you guess his favorite team?

Birthdate: May 15, 1995
Price Paid: $_____
Date Purchased: _____
Tag Generation: _____

123

Snowball™

Snowman · #4201
Issued: October 1, 1997
Retired: December 31, 1997

Market Value:
❹–$55

Birthdate: December 22, 1996
Price Paid: $_____
Date Purchased: _____
Tag Generation: _____

There is a snowman, I've been told
That plays with Beanies out in the cold
What is better in a winter wonderland
Than a Beanie snowman in your hand!

124

Sparky™

Dalmatian · #4100
Issued: June 15, 1996
Retired: May 11, 1997

Market Value:
❹–$160

Birthdate: February 27, 1996
Price Paid: $_____
Date Purchased: _____
Tag Generation: _____

Sparky rides proud on the fire truck
Ringing the bell and pushing his luck
He gets under foot when trying to help
He often gets stepped on and
Lets out a yelp!

Value
Totals _____

COLLECTOR'S
VALUE GUIDE™

125

Speedy™

Turtle · #4030
Issued: June 25, 1994
Retired: October 1, 1997

Market Value:
❹- $40
❸- $130
❷- $255
❶- $350

Speedy ran marathons in the past
Such a shame, always last
Now Speedy is a big star
After he bought a racing car!

Birthdate: August 14, 1994
Price Paid: $_____
Date Purchased: _____
Tag Generation: _____

126

Spike™

Rhinoceros · #4060
Issued: June 15, 1996
Current – Easy To Find

Market Value:
❺- $_____
❹- $14

Spike the rhino likes to stampede
He's the bruiser that you need
Gentle to birds on his back and spike
You can be his friend if you like!

Birthdate: August 13, 1996
Price Paid: $_____
Date Purchased: _____
Tag Generation: _____

127

B

The Beanie Babies Collection®

ty

Creepy
HANDMADE IN CHINA
© 1996 TY INC.
OAKBROOK, IL U.S.A.
SURFACE WASHABLE
ALL NEW MATERIAL
POLYESTER FIBER
& PVC PELLETS CE
REG. NO. PA. 1965(KR)

A

ty

Spinner™

Spider • #4036
Issued: October 1, 1997
Retired: September 19, 1998

Market Value:
A. "Spinner™" Tush Tag
(Oct. 97-Sept. 98)
⑤- $12
④- $18
B. "Creepy™" Tush Tag
(Est. Late 97-Sept. 98)
⑤- $60

Birthdate: October 28, 1996
Price Paid: $_____
Date Purchased: _____
Tag Generation: _____

Does this spider make you scared?
Among many people that feeling is shared
Remember spiders have feelings too
In fact, this spider really likes you!

128

9
ORIGINAL
NINE

Splash™

Whale • #4022
Issued: January 8, 1994
Retired: May 11, 1997

Market Value:
④- $140
③- $225
②- $400
①- $490

Birthdate: July 8, 1993
Price Paid: $_____
Date Purchased: _____
Tag Generation: _____

Splash loves to jump and dive
He's the fastest whale alive
He always wins the 100 yard dash
With a victory jump he'll make a splash!

Value
Totals _____

COLLECTOR'S
VALUE GUIDE™

Spooky™

Ghost • #4090
Issued: September 1, 1995
Retired: December 31, 1997

Market Value:

A. "Spooky™" Swing Tag
(Est. Late 95-Dec. 97)
④- $42
③- $140

B. "Spook™" Swing Tag
(Est. Sept. 95-Late 95)
③- $425

B

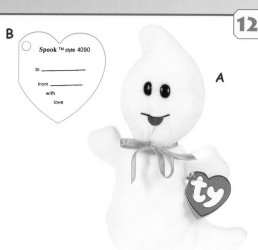

Spook ™ style 4090

to _____

from _____

with

love

A

Ghosts can be a scary sight
But don't let Spooky bring you any fright
Because when you're alone, you will see
The best friend that Spooky can be!

Birthdate: October 31, 1995
Price Paid: $_____
Date Purchased: _____
Tag Generation: _____

Spot™

Dog • #4000
Issued: January 8, 1994
Retired: October 1, 1997

Market Value:

A. With Spot
(April 94-Oct. 97)
④- $60
③- $150
②- $865

B. Without Spot
(Jan. 94–April 94)
②- $2,100
①- $2,200

B

A

ORIGINAL NINE

See Spot sprint, see Spot run
You and Spot will have lots of fun
Watch out now, because he's not slow
Just stand back and watch him go!

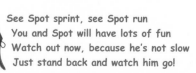

Birthdate: January 3, 1993
Price Paid: $_____
Date Purchased: _____
Tag Generation: _____

COLLECTOR'S
VALUE GUIDE™

Value
Totals _____

131

Spunky™

Cocker Spaniel · #4184
Issued: December 31, 1997
Current – Easy To Find

Market Value:
5 - $_____

Birthdate: January 14, 1997
Price Paid: $_____
Date Purchased: _____
Tag Generation: _____

Bouncing around without much grace
To jump on your lap and lick your face
But watch him closely he has no fears
He'll run so fast he'll trip over his ears

132

ORIGINAL NINE

Squealer™

Pig · #4005
Issued: January 8, 1994
Retired: May 1, 1998

Market Value:
5 - $35
4 - $40
3 - $125
2 - $260
1 - $350

Birthdate: April 23, 1993
Price Paid: $_____
Date Purchased: _____
Tag Generation: _____

Squealer likes to joke around
He is known as class clown
Listen to his stories awhile
There is no doubt he'll make you smile!

Value Totals _____

COLLECTOR'S
VALUE GUIDE™

Steg™

133

Stegosaurus · #4087
Issued: June 3, 1995
Retired: June 15, 1996

Market Value:
❸–$1,025

No Poem_____
_____
_____
_____

Birthdate: N/A
Price Paid: $_____
Date Purchased: _____
Tag Generation: _____

134

Sting™

Stingray · #4077
Issued: June 3, 1995
Retired: January 1, 1997

Market Value:
❹–$210
❸–$280

I'm a manta ray and my name is Sting
I'm quite unusual and this is the thing
Under the water I glide like a bird
Have you ever seen something so absurd?

Birthdate: August 27, 1995
Price Paid: $_____
Date Purchased: _____
Tag Generation: _____

135

Stinger™

Scorpion • #4193
Issued: May 30, 1998
Current – Moderate To Find

Market Value:
❺- $_____

Birthdate: September 29, 1997
Price Paid: $_____
Date Purchased: _____
Tag Generation: _____

Stinger the scorpion will run and dart
But this little fellow is really all heart
So if you see him don't run away
Say hello and ask him to play!

136

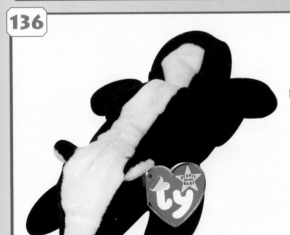

Stinky™

Skunk • #4017
Issued: June 3, 1995
Retired: September 28, 1998

Market Value:
❺- $14
❹- $17
❸- $100

Birthdate: February 13, 1995
Price Paid: $_____
Date Purchased: _____
Tag Generation: _____

Deep in the woods he lived in a cave
Perfume and mints were the gifts he gave
He showered every night in the kitchen sink
Hoping one day he wouldn't stink!

Value
Totals _____

COLLECTOR'S
VALUE GUIDE™

Stretch™

137

Ostrich · #4182
Issued: December 31, 1997
Current – Easy To Find

Market Value:
⑤- $_____

She thinks when her head is underground
The rest of her body can't be found
The Beanie Babies think it's absurd
To play hide and seek with this bird!

Birthdate: September 21, 1997
Price Paid: $_____
Date Purchased: _____
Tag Generation: _____

Stripes™

138

Tiger · #4065
Issued: Est. June 3, 1995
Retired: May 1, 1998

Market Value:
A. Light w/Fewer Stripes
(June 96-May 98)
⑤- $22
④- $26
B. Dark w/Fuzzy Belly
(Est. Early 96-June 96)
③- $1,000
C. Dark w/More Stripes
(Est. June 95-Early 96)
③- $375

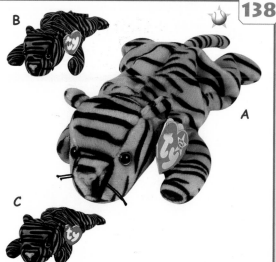

B

A

C

Stripes was never fierce nor strong
So with tigers, he didn't get along
Jungle life was hard to get by
So he came to his friends at Ty!

Birthdate: June 11, 1995
Price Paid: $_____
Date Purchased: _____
Tag Generation: _____

Value
Totals _____

139

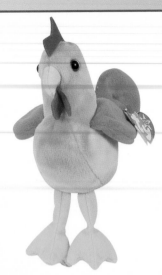

Strut™
(name changed from "Doodle™")

Rooster · #4171
Issued: July 12, 1997
Current – Easy To Find

Market Value:
⑤- $_____
④- $20

Birthdate: March 8, 1996
Price Paid: $_____
Date Purchased: _____
Tag Generation: _____

Listen closely to "cock-a-doodle-doo"
What's the rooster saying to you?
Hurry, wake up sleepy head
We have lots to do, get out of bed!

140

Tabasco™

Bull · #4002
Issued: June 3, 1995
Retired: January 1, 1997

Market Value:
④- $215
③- $280

Birthdate: May 15, 1995
Price Paid: $_____
Date Purchased: _____
Tag Generation: _____

Although Tabasco is not so tall
He loves to play basketball
He is a star player in his dream
Can you guess his favorite team?

Value
Totals _____

COLLECTOR'S
VALUE GUIDE™

141

Tank™

Armadillo · #4031
Issued: Est. January 7, 1996
Retired: October 1, 1997

Market Value:
A. 9 Plates/With Shell
   (Est. Late 96-Oct. 97)
   ④-$78
B. 9 Plates/Without Shell
   (Est. Mid 96-Late 96)
   ④-$210
C. 7 Plates/Without Shell
   (Est. Jan. 96-Mid 96)
   ③-$200

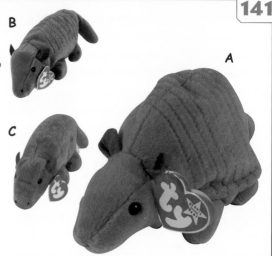

This armadillo lives in the South
Shoving Tex-Mex in his mouth
He sure loves it south of the border
Keeping his friends in good order!

Birthdate: February 22, 1995
Price Paid: $_____
Date Purchased: _____
Tag Generation: _____

142

Teddy™ (brown)

Bear · #4050
Issued: June 25, 1994
Retired: October 1, 1997

Market Value:
A. New Face (Jan. 95-Oct. 97)
   ④-$105
   ③-$375
   ②-$950
B. Old Face (June 94-Jan. 95)
   ②-$2,900
   ①-$3,100

Teddy wanted to go out today
All of his friends went out to play
But he'd rather help whatever you do
After all, his best friend is you!

Birthdate: November 28, 1995
Price Paid: $_____
Date Purchased: _____
Tag Generation: _____

COLLECTOR'S
VALUE GUIDE™

Value
Totals _____

143

B

A

Teddy™ (cranberry)

Bear • #4052
Issued: June 25, 1994
Retired: January 7, 1996

Market Value:
A. New Face (Jan. 95-Jan. 96)
❸ - $1,900
❷ - $2,000
B. Old Face (June 94-Jan. 95)
❷ - $1,900
❶ - $2,000

Birthdate: N/A
Price Paid: $_____
Date Purchased: _____
Tag Generation: _____

No Poem_____
_____
_____
_____

144

B

A

Teddy™ (jade)

Bear • #4057
Issued: June 25, 1994
Retired: January 7, 1996

Market Value:
A. New Face (Jan. 95-Jan. 96)
❸ - $1,900
❷ - $2,000
B. Old Face (June 94-Jan. 95)
❷ - $1,800
❶ - $1,900

Birthdate: N/A
Price Paid: $_____
Date Purchased: _____
Tag Generation: _____

No Poem_____
_____
_____
_____

Value
Totals _____

COLLECTOR'S
VALUE GUIDE™

145

Teddy™ (magenta)

B  A

Bear · #4056
Issued: June 25, 1994
Retired: January 7, 1996

Market Value:
A. New Face (Jan. 95-Jan. 96)
❸- $1,900
❷- $2,000
B. Old Face (June 94-Jan. 95)
❷- $1,800
❶- $1,900

No Poem_____
_____
_____
_____

Birthdate: N/A
Price Paid: $_____
Date Purchased: _____
Tag Generation: _____

146

Teddy™ (teal)

B 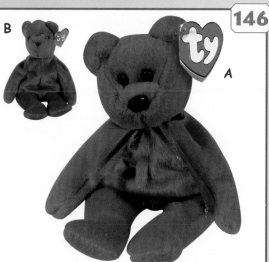 A

Bear · #4051
Issued: June 25, 1994
Retired: January 7, 1996

Market Value:
A. New Face (Jan. 95-Jan. 96)
❸- $1,900
❷- $2,000
B. Old Face (June 94-Jan. 95)
❷- $1,800
❶- $1,900

No Poem_____
_____
_____
_____

Birthdate: N/A
Price Paid: $_____
Date Purchased: _____
Tag Generation: _____

147

A

B

C

Teddy™ (violet)

Bear · #4055
Issued: June 25, 1994
Retired: January 7, 1996

Market Value:
A. New Face (Jan. 95-Jan. 96)
 ❸ – $1,900
 ❷ – $2,000
B. New Face/Employee Bear
 w/Red Tush Tag
 (Green or Red Ribbon)
 No Swing Tag – $4,000
C. Old Face (June 94-Jan. 95)
 ❷ – $1,800
 ❶ – $1,900

Birthdate: N/A
Price Paid: $_____
Date Purchased: _____
Tag Generation: _____

No Poem_____
_____
_____
_____

148

Tracker™

Basset Hound · #4198
Issued: May 30, 1998
Current – Moderate To Find

Market Value:
❺ – $_____

Birthdate: June 5, 1997
Price Paid: $_____
Date Purchased: _____
Tag Generation: _____

Sniffing and tracking and following trails
Tracker the basset always wags his tail
It doesn't matter what you do
He's always happy when he's with you!

Value
Totals _____

COLLECTOR'S
VALUE GUIDE™

149

Trap™

Mouse · #4042
Issued: June 25, 1994
Retired: June 15, 1995

Market Value:
- ❸- $1,575
- ❷- $1,650
- ❶- $1,850

No Poem_____
_____
_____

Birthdate: N/A
Price Paid: $_____
Date Purchased: _____
Tag Generation: _____

150

Tuffy™

Terrier · #4108
Issued: May 11, 1997
Current – Easy To Find

Market Value:
- ❺- $_____
- ❹- $14

Taking off with a thunderous blast
Tuffy rides his motorcycle fast
The Beanies roll with laughs and squeals
He never took off his training wheels!

Birthdate: October 12, 1996
Price Paid: $_____
Date Purchased: _____
Tag Generation: _____

151

B

Tuck™ style 4076
DATE OF BIRTH : 9 - 18 - 95
Tusk brushes his teeth everyday
To keep them shiny, it's the only way
Teeth are special, so you must try
To sparkle when you say 'Hi'!
Visit our web page!!!
http://www.ty.com

A

Tusk™

Walrus · #4076
Issued: Est. June 3, 1995
Retired: January 1, 1997

Market Value:
A. "Tusk™" Swing Tag
(Est. June 95-Jan. 97)
❹ – $155
❸ – $240
B. "Tuck™" Swing Tag
(Est. Early 96-Jan. 97)
❹ – $175

Birthdate: September 18, 1995
Price Paid: $_____
Date Purchased: _____
Tag Generation: _____

Tusk brushes his teeth everyday
To keep them shiny, it's the only way
Teeth are special, so you must try
And they will sparkle when
You say "Hi"!

152

Twigs™

Giraffe · #4068
Issued: January 7, 1996
Retired: May 1, 1998

Market Value:
❺ – $27
❹ – $30
❸ – $120

Birthdate: May 19, 1995
Price Paid: $_____
Date Purchased: _____
Tag Generation: _____

Twigs has his head in the clouds
He stands tall, he stands proud
With legs so skinny they wobble and shake
What an unusual friend he will make!

Value Totals _____

COLLECTOR'S
VALUE GUIDE™

Valentino™

Bear · #4058
Issued: January 7, 1995
Current – Hard To Find

Market Value:
⑤-$_____
④-$33
③-$140
②-$250

153

His heart is red and full of love
He cares for you so give him a hug
Keep him close when feeling blue
Feel the love he has for you!

Birthdate: February 14, 1994
Price Paid: $_____
Date Purchased: _____
Tag Generation: _____

Velvet™

Panther · #4064
Issued: June 3, 1995
Retired: October 1, 1997

Market Value:
④-$38
③-$125

154

Velvet loves to sleep in the trees
Lulled to dreams by the buzz of the bees
She snoozes all day and plays all night
Running and jumping in the moonlight!

Birthdate: December 16, 1995
Price Paid: $_____
Date Purchased: _____
Tag Generation: _____

COLLECTOR'S
VALUE GUIDE™

Value
Totals _____

155

Waddle™

Penguin · #4075
Issued: June 3, 1995
Retired: May 1, 1998

Market Value:
- 5 - $25
- 4 - $30
- 3 - $115

Birthdate: December 19, 1995
Price Paid: $_____
Date Purchased: _____
Tag Generation: _____

Waddle the Penguin likes to dress up
Every night he wears his tux
When Waddle walks, it never fails
He always trips over his tails!

156

Waves™

Whale · #4084
Issued: May 11, 1997
Retired: May 1, 1998

Market Value:
- 5 - $23
- 4 - $28

Birthdate: December 8, 1996
Price Paid: $_____
Date Purchased: _____
Tag Generation: _____

Join him today on the Internet
Don't be afraid to get your feet wet
He taught all the Beanies how to surf
Our web page is his home turf!

Value
Totals _____

COLLECTOR'S
VALUE GUIDE™

Web™

Spider · #4041
Issued: June 25, 1994
Retired: January 7, 1996

Market Value:
3 - $1,550
2 - $1,650
1 - $1,800

No Poem_____

_____

_____

Birthdate: N/A
Price Paid: $_____
Date Purchased: _____
Tag Generation: _____

Weenie™

Dachshund · #4013
Issued: January 7, 1996
Retired: May 1, 1998

Market Value:
5 - $33
4 - $38
3 - $130

TOP DOG

Weenie the dog is quite a sight
Long of body and short of height
He perches himself high on a log
And considers himself to be top dog!

Birthdate: July 20, 1995
Price Paid: $_____
Date Purchased: _____
Tag Generation: _____

COLLECTOR'S
VALUE GUIDE™

Value
Totals _____

159

Whisper™

Deer • #4194
Issued: May 30, 1998
Current – Moderate To Find

Market Value:
🖤- $_____

Birthdate: April 5, 1997
Price Paid: $_____
Date Purchased: _____
Tag Generation: _____

She's very shy as you can see
When she hides behind a tree
With big brown eyes and soft to touch
This little fawn will love you so much!

160

Wise™

Owl • #4187
Issued: May 30, 1998
Current – Hard To Find

Market Value:
🖤- $_____

Birthdate: May 31, 1997
Price Paid: $_____
Date Purchased: _____
Tag Generation: _____

Wise is at the head of the class
With A's and B's he'll always pass
He's got his diploma and feels really great
Meet the newest graduate: Class of '98!

Value
Totals _____

Wrinkles™

Bulldog · #4103
Issued: June 15, 1996
Retired: September 22, 1998

Market Value:
- ⑤- $15
- ④- $20

This little dog is named Wrinkles
His nose is soft and often crinkles
Likes to climb up on your lap
He's a cheery sort of chap!

Birthdate: May 1, 1996
Price Paid: $_____
Date Purchased: _____
Tag Generation: _____

Zero™

NEW!

Penguin · #4207
Issued: September 30, 1998
Current – Just Released

Market Value:
- ⑤- $_____

Penguins love the ice and snow
Playing in weather twenty below
Antarctica is where I love to be
Splashing in the cold, cold sea!

Birthdate: January 2, 1998
Price Paid: $_____
Date Purchased: _____
Tag Generation: _____

COLLECTOR'S
VALUE GUIDE™

Value
Totals _____

163

Ziggy™

Zebra · #4063
Issued: June 3, 1995
Retired: May 1, 1998

Market Value:
❺– $30
❹– $34
❸– $120

Birthdate: December 24, 1995
Price Paid: $_____
Date Purchased: _____
Tag Generation: _____

Ziggy likes soccer – he's a referee
That way he watches the games for free
The other Beanies don't think it's fair
But Ziggy the Zebra doesn't care!

164

Zip™

Cat · #4004
Issued: January 7, 1995
Retired: May 1, 1998

Market Value:
A. White Paws
(March 96-May 98)
❺– $50 ❹– $55 ❸– $575
B. All Black
(Jan. 96-March 96)
❸– $1,950
C. White Face
(Jan. 95-Jan. 96)
❸– $575 ❷– $600

A
B
C

Birthdate: March 28, 1994
Price Paid: $_____
Date Purchased: _____
Tag Generation: _____

Keep Zip by your side all the day through
Zip is good luck, you'll see it's true
When you have something you need to do
Zip will always believe in you!

Value Totals _____

COLLECTOR'S
VALUE GUIDE™

SPORTS PROMOTION BEANIE BABIES®

The Sports Promotion *Beanie Babies* have scored points among collectors and sports fans alike. Originally introduced in hopes of increasing attendance at specific sporting events, these *Beanie Babies* with their official commemorative cards have attracted a lot of attention on the secondary market. Some collectors even seek out the ticket stubs! Here's a rundown of some of the special *Beanie Babies* sports promotions announced through October 1998.

A friend to many. A legend to all
The most popular figure in all of baseball
Crowds would cheer when hearing his name
Without you Harry, it won't be the same

In memory of Harry Caray
Ty presents Daisy™
at Wrigley Field
May 3, 1998

SPORTS PROMOTION BEANIE BABIES® KEY

 Canadian Special Olympics

 National Football League

 Major League Baseball

 National Hockey League

 National Basketball Association

 Women's National Basketball Association

	Baldy™		Batty™		Batty™
1	Philadelphia 76ers 1/17/98 · LE-5,000 Market Value: $240	**2**	Milwaukee Brewers 5/31/98 · LE-12,000 Market Value: $170	**3**	New York Mets 7/12/98 · LE-30,000 Market Value: $170
4	Blackie™ Boston Bruins 10/12/98 · LE-5,000 Market Value: N/E	**5**	Blackie™ Chicago Bears In Club Kits · LE-20,000 Market Value: $80	**6**	Blackie™ Chicago Bears 11/8/98 · LE-8,000 Market Value: N/E
7	Blizzard™ Chicago White Sox 7/12/98 · LE-20,000 Market Value: $170	**8**	Bones™ Chicago Blackhawks 10/24/98 · LE-5,000 Market Value: N/E	**9**	Bones™ New York Yankees 3/10/98 · N/A Market Value: $250

SPORTS PROMOTION BEANIE BABIES®

	Price Paid	Value of My Collection
1.		
2.		
3.		
4.		
5.		
6.		
7.		
8.		
9.		

Value Totals _____

VALUE GUIDE — SPORTS PROMOTION BEANIE BABIES®

10

Bongo™
Charlotte Sting
7/17/98 · LE-3,000
Market Value: $220

11
Bongo™
Cleveland Cavaliers
4/5/98 · LE-5,000
Market Value: $220

12
Chip™
Atlanta Braves
8/19/98 · LE-12,000
Market Value: $95

13

Chocolate™
Dallas Cowboys
9/6/98 · LE-10,000
Market Value: $120

14

Chocolate™
Denver Nuggets
4/17/98 · LE-5,000
Market Value: $220

15
Chocolate™
Seattle Mariners
9/5/98 · LE-10,000
Market Value: $65

16

Chocolate™
Tennessee Oilers
10/18/98 · LE-7,500
Market Value: N/E

17

Cubbie™
Chicago Cubs
1/16-1/18/98 · LE-100
Market Value: $500

18
Cubbie™
Chicago Cubs
5/18/97 · LE-10,000
Market Value: $215

19
Cubbie™
Chicago Cubs
9/6/97 · LE-10,000
Market Value: $180

20
Curly™
Charlotte Sting
6/15/98 · LE-5,000
Market Value: $230

21
Curly™
Chicago Bears
12/20/98 · LE-10,000
Market Value: N/E

SPORTS PROMOTION BEANIE BABIES®		
	Price Paid	Value of My Collection
10.		
11.		
12.		
13.		
14.		
15.		
16.		
17.		
18.		
19.		
20.		
21.		
22.		
23.		
24.		
25.		
26.		
27.		
28.		
29.		
30.		
31.		
32.		
33.		
34.		
35.		
36.		

22

Curly™
Cleveland Rockers
8/15/98 · LE-3,200
Market Value: $130

23
Curly™
New York Mets
8/22/98 · LE-30,000
Market Value: $75

24
Curly™
San Antonio Spurs
4/27/98 · LE-2,500
Market Value: $250

25
Daisy™
Chicago Cubs
5/3/98 · LE-10,000
Market Value: $460

26
Derby™
Houston Astros
8/16/98 · LE-15,000
Market Value: $105

27
Dotty™
Los Angeles Sparks
7/31/98 · LE-3,000
Market Value: $170

28
Ears™
Oakland A's
3/15/98 · LE-1,500
Market Value: $275

29
Glory™
All-Star Game
7/7/98 · LE-52,000 approx.
Market Value: $380

30

Gobbles™
St. Louis Blues
11/24/98 · LE-7,500
Market Value: N/E

31
Gracie™
Chicago Cubs
9/13/98 · LE-10,000
Market Value: $200

32
Hissy™
Arizona Diamondbacks
6/14/98 · LE-6,500
Market Value: $175

33
Lucky™
Minnesota Twins
7/31/98 · LE-10,000
Market Value: $190

34

Maple™
Canadian Special Olympics
8/97 & 12/97 · N/A
Market Value: $575

35
Mel™
Anaheim Angels
9/6/98 · LE-10,000
Market Value: $80

36

Mel™
Detroit Shock
7/25/98 · LE-5,000
Market Value: $150

Value Totals _____

COLLECTOR'S
VALUE GUIDE™

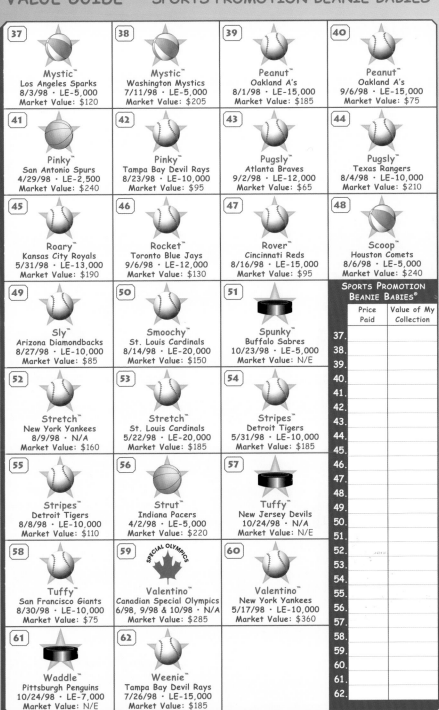

37 Mystic™
Los Angeles Sparks
8/3/98 · LE-5,000
Market Value: $120

38 Mystic™
Washington Mystics
7/11/98 · LE-5,000
Market Value: $205

39 Peanut™
Oakland A's
8/1/98 · LE-15,000
Market Value: $185

40 Peanut™
Oakland A's
9/6/98 · LE-15,000
Market Value: $75

41 Pinky™
San Antonio Spurs
4/29/98 · LE-2,500
Market Value: $240

42 Pinky™
Tampa Bay Devil Rays
8/23/98 · LE-10,000
Market Value: $95

43 Pugsly™
Atlanta Braves
9/2/98 · LE-12,000
Market Value: $65

44 Pugsly™
Texas Rangers
8/4/98 · LE-10,000
Market Value: $210

45 Roary™
Kansas City Royals
5/31/98 · LE-13,000
Market Value: $190

46 Rocket™
Toronto Blue Jays
9/6/98 · LE-12,000
Market Value: $130

47 Rover™
Cincinnati Reds
8/16/98 · LE-15,000
Market Value: $95

48 Scoop™
Houston Comets
8/6/98 · LE-5,000
Market Value: $240

49 Sly™
Arizona Diamondbacks
8/27/98 · LE-10,000
Market Value: $85

50 Smoochy™
St. Louis Cardinals
8/14/98 · LE-20,000
Market Value: $150

51 Spunky™
Buffalo Sabres
10/23/98 · LE-5,000
Market Value: N/E

52 Stretch™
New York Yankees
8/9/98 · N/A
Market Value: $160

53 Stretch™
St. Louis Cardinals
5/22/98 · LE-20,000
Market Value: $185

54 Stripes™
Detroit Tigers
5/31/98 · LE-10,000
Market Value: $185

55 Stripes™
Detroit Tigers
8/8/98 · LE-10,000
Market Value: $110

56 Strut™
Indiana Pacers
4/2/98 · LE-5,000
Market Value: $220

57 Tuffy™
New Jersey Devils
10/24/98 · N/A
Market Value: N/E

58 Tuffy™
San Francisco Giants
8/30/98 · LE-10,000
Market Value: $75

59 Valentino™
Canadian Special Olympics
6/98, 9/98 & 10/98 · N/A
Market Value: $285

60 Valentino™
New York Yankees
5/17/98 · LE-10,000
Market Value: $360

61 Waddle™
Pittsburgh Penguins
10/24/98 · LE-7,000
Market Value: N/E

62 Weenie™
Tampa Bay Devil Rays
7/26/98 · LE-15,000
Market Value: $185

SPORTS PROMOTION BEANIE BABIES®		
	Price Paid	Value of My Collection
37.		
38.		
39.		
40.		
41.		
42.		
43.		
44.		
45.		
46.		
47.		
48.		
49.		
50.		
51.		
52.		
53.		
54.		
55.		
56.		
57.		
58.		
59.		
60.		
61.		
62.		

COLLECTOR'S
VALUE GUIDE™

Value Totals _____

INTRODUCING THE BEANIE BUDDIES®

On September 30, 1998, Ty announced a whole new collectible line featuring several familiar faces – the *Beanie Buddies*! The *Beanie Buddies* are a little bit larger than their *Beanie Babies* counterparts and are made of a special new fabric. Among the nine interesting new designs are larger versions of three very valuable *Beanie Babies*: "Humphrey" the camel, "Teddy" the cranberry bear and "Peanut" the dark blue elephant.

1

NEW!

Beak™

Kiwi • #9301
Issued: September 30, 1998
Current – Just Released

Market Value: $_____

Beanie Buddies® Fact
Beak the Beanie Baby
and Beak the Beanie Buddy
are the first to be released as a set!

F.Y.I.

Price Paid: $_____
Date Purchased: _____

Value
Totals _____

COLLECTOR'S
VALUE GUIDE™

2

NEW!

Humphrey™

Camel · #9307
Issued: September 30, 1998
Current – Just Released

Market Value: $_____

Beanie Buddies® Fact
Humphrey the Beanie Baby
was one of the first to be retired.
Very few were produced,
making him highly collectable!

Price Paid: $_____
Date Purchased: _____

3

NEW!

Jake™

Mallard Duck · #9304
Issued: September 30, 1998
Current – Just Released

Market Value: $_____

Beanie Buddies® Fact
Jake the Beanie Baby
due to his numerous colors
was difficult to manufacture
making him one of the most sought after!

Price Paid: $_____
Date Purchased: _____

4

NEW!

Peanut™

Elephant · #9300
Issued: September 30, 1998
Current – Just Released

Market Value: $_____

Price Paid: $_____
Date Purchased: _____

Beanie Buddies® Fact
Peanut the Beanie Baby
made in this royal blue color
is extremely rare and very valuable!

5

NEW!

Quackers™

Duck · #9302
Issued: September 30, 199?
Current – Just Released

Market Value: $____

Price Paid: $_____
Date Purchased: _____

Beanie Buddies® Fact
Quackers the Beanie Baby
retired in May 1998,
was once made without wings!

F.Y.I.

Value
Totals _____

COLLECTOR'S
VALUE GUIDE™

6

Rover™

Dog · #9305
Issued: September 30, 1998
Current – Just Released

Market Value: $_____

Beanie Buddies® Fact
Rover the Beanie Baby
was the first non-breed dog.
Introduced in the summer of 1996
this red color set him apart!

F.Y.I.

Price Paid: $_____
Date Purchased: _____

7

Stretch™

Ostrich · #9303
Issued: September 30, 1998
Current – Just Released

Market Value: $_____

Beanie Buddies® Fact
Stretch the Beanie Baby
is one of the most difficult to p[ ]
due to her long neck and numerou[ ]

F.Y.I.

Price Paid: $_____
Date Purchased: _____

Value
Totals _____

8

NEW!

Teddy™

Bear · #9306
Issued: September 30, 1998
Current – Just Released

Market Value: $_____

Beanie Buddies® Fact
Teddy the Beanie Baby
was made in six colors.
A very limited number were produced
in this special cranberry color!

Price Paid: $_____
Date Purchased: _____

9

NEW!

Twigs™

Giraffe · #9308
Issued: September 30, 1998
Current – Just Released

Market Value: $_____

Beanie Buddies® Fact
Twigs the Beanie Baby
was manufactured in fabric
created exclusively for Ty
and was retired in May 1998!

Price Paid: $_____
Date Purchased: _____

Value
Totals _____

COLLECTOR'S
VALUE GUIDE™

TB1

1997 Teenie Beanie Babies™ Complete Set (set/10)
Issued: April 11, 1997
Retired: May 15, 1997
Price Paid: $_____
Market Value: $240

TB2

1998 Teenie Beanie Babies™ Complete Set (set/12)
Issued: May 22, 1998
Retired: June 12, 1998
Price Paid: $_____
Market Value: $90

TB3

Bones™
Dog • 2nd Promotion, #9 of 12
Issued: May 22, 1998
Retired: June 12, 1998
Price Paid: $_____
Market Value: $9

TB4

Bongo™
Monkey • 2nd Promotion, #2 of 12
Issued: May 22, 1998
Retired: June 12, 1998
Price Paid: $_____
Market Value: $15

TB5

Chocolate™
Moose • 1st Promotion, #4 of 10
Issued: April 11, 1997
Retired: May 15, 1997
Price Paid: $_____
Market Value: $35

TB6

Chops™
Lamb • 1st Promotion, #3 of 10
Issued: April 11, 1997
Retired: May 15, 1997
Price Paid: $_____
Market Value: $38

COLLECTOR'S
VALUE GUIDE™

Value Totals _____

TB7

Doby™
Doberman • 2nd Promotion, #1 of 12
Issued: May 22, 1998
Retired: June 12, 1998
Price Paid: $_____
Market Value: $17

TB8

Goldie™
Goldfish • 1st Promotion, #5 of 10
Issued: April 11, 1997
Retired: May 15, 1997
Price Paid: $_____
Market Value: $28

TB9

Happy™
Hippo • 2nd Promotion, #6 of 12
Issued: May 22, 1998
Retired: June 12, 1998
Price Paid: $_____
Market Value: $9

TB10

Inch™
Inchworm • 2nd Promotion, #4 of 12
Issued: May 22, 1998
Retired: June 12, 1998
Price Paid: $_____
Market Value: $9

TB11

Lizz™
Lizard • 1st Promotion, #10 of 10
Issued: April 11, 1997
Retired: May 15, 1997
Price Paid: $_____
Market Value: $22

TB12

Mel™
Koala • 2nd Promotion, #7 of 12
Issued: May 22, 1998
Retired: June 12, 1998
Price Paid: $_____
Market Value: $9

Value
Totals _____

TB13

Patti™
Platypus • 1st Promotion, #1 of 10
Issued: April 11, 1997
Retired: May 15, 1997
Price Paid: $_____
Market Value: $42

TB14

Peanut™
Elephant • 2nd Promotion, #12 of 12
Issued: May 22, 1998
Retired: June 12, 1998
Price Paid: $_____
Market Value: $10

TB15

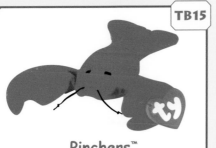

Pinchers™
Lobster • 2nd Promotion, #5 of 12
Issued: May 22, 1998
Retired: June 12, 1998
Price Paid: $_____
Market Value: $9

TB16

Pinky™
Flamingo • 1st Promotion, #2 of 10
Issued: April 11, 1997
Retired: May 15, 1997
Price Paid: $_____
Market Value: $50

TB17

Quacks™
Duck • 1st Promotion, #9 of 10
Issued: April 11, 1997
Retired: May 15, 1997
Price Paid: $_____
Market Value: $22

TB18

Scoop™
Pelican • 2nd Promotion, #8 of 12
Issued: May 22, 1998
Retired: June 12, 1998
Price Paid: $_____
Market Value: $9

TB19

Seamore™
Seal · 1st Promotion, #7 of 10
Issued: April 11, 1997
Retired: May 15, 1997
Price Paid: $_____
Market Value: $32

TB20

Snort™
Bull · 1st Promotion, #8 of 10
Issued: April 11, 1997
Retired: May 15, 1997
Price Paid: $_____
Market Value: $21

TB21

Speedy™
Turtle · 1st Promotion, #6 of 10
Issued: April 11, 1997
Retired: May 15, 1997
Price Paid: $_____
Market Value: $28

TB22

Twigs™
Giraffe · 2nd Promotion, #3 of 12
Issued: May 22, 1998
Retired: June 12, 1998
Price Paid: $_____
Market Value: $12

TB23

Waddle™
Penguin · 2nd Promotion, #11 of 12
Issued: May 22, 1998
Retired: June 12, 1998
Price Paid: $_____
Market Value: $10

TB24

Zip™
Cat · 2nd Promotion, #10 of 12
Issued: May 22, 1998
Retired: June 12, 1998
Price Paid: $_____
Market Value: $10

Value
Totals _____

COLLECTOR'S
VALUE GUIDE™

TOTAL VALUE OF MY COLLECTION

BEANIE BABIES® VALUE TOTALS	BEANIE BABIES® VALUE TOTALS	BEANIE BABIES® VALUE TOTALS
Page 25	Page 61	Page 97
Page 26	Page 62	Page 98
Page 27	Page 63	Page 99
Page 28	Page 64	Page 100
Page 29	Page 65	Page 101
Page 30	Page 66	Page 102
Page 31	Page 67	Page 103
Page 32	Page 68	Page 104
Page 33	Page 69	Page 105
Page 34	Page 70	Page 106
Page 35	Page 71	Subtotal
Page 36	Page 72	**SPORTS PROMOTION BEANIE BABIES® VALUE TOTALS**
Page 37	Page 73	Page 107
Page 38	Page 74	Page 108
Page 39	Page 75	Page 109
Page 40	Page 76	Subtotal
Page 41	Page 77	**BEANIE BUDDIES® VALUE TOTALS**
Page 42	Page 78	Page 110
Page 43	Page 79	Page 111
Page 44	Page 80	Page 112
Page 45	Page 81	Page 113
Page 46	Page 82	Page 114
Page 47	Page 83	Subtotal
Page 48	Page 84	**TEENIE BEANIE BABIES™ VALUE TOTALS**
Page 49	Page 85	Page 115
Page 50	Page 86	Page 116
Page 51	Page 87	Page 117
Page 52	Page 88	Page 118
Page 53	Page 89	Subtotal
Page 54	Page 90	
Page 55	Page 91	
Page 56	Page 92	
Page 57	Page 93	
Page 58	Page 94	
Page 59	Page 95	
Page 60	Page 96	

COLLECTOR'S
VALUE GUIDE™

Grand Totals _____

*F*or many people, the motivation behind venturing into the wilderness of the *Beanie Babies* was for the happiness that the critters would bring. And it is for this exact reason that they were first introduced by Ty Inc. But the cute little animals surpassed all expectations and *Beanie Babies* were catapulted from the world of stuffed toys into the world of collectibles. Today, it is hard to imagine anyone who is not aware of the *Beanie Babies* craze and that, in itself, illustrates the effect that these beanbag animals have had on the industry.

As more people began seeing the *Beanie Babies* as collectibles, they found out there was a whole *Beanie Babies* world out there, including many pieces that they didn't have. And when they went to their local store to purchase these missing pieces, they unfortunately found out that many had already been retired. It seemed like it would take nothing less than magic to find these animals. Then collectors discovered the charm of the *Beanie Babies* secondary market.

WHAT'S FOR SALE AT THIS MARKET?

Most "hot" collectibles have been around for a long time and appreciate in value very gradually. *Beanie Babies* however, which have only been available for about five years, have single-handedly revolutionized the traditional collectibles secondary market. Normally, the secondary market for a collectible is created when a piece is retired (removed from production) and is no longer available in stores. This standard certainly applies to *Beanie Babies*, as the retired pieces are among the most valuable pieces in the collection.

However, in a trend unique to this line, an additional demand has been created for the pieces that are still currently being produced – with some of the more recent releases and the ever-popular bear designs being nearly *impossible* to locate on store shelves.

There are several reasons for this occurrence. First, as the demand for the *Beanie Babies* skyrockets, production is often not able to keep up. Consequently, shipment to stores is slowed, sending anxious collectors on a quest to find these current pieces. Sometimes, these collectors turn to the secondary market where they will pay inflated prices for pieces that will eventually appear in stores at a much lower retail price.

The swing tag generations also play a crucial role in the secondary market value of current (and retired) pieces (see section on tags on page 18). While "Chocolate" with a fifth generation swing tag may be on the shelves of every store across America, "Chocolate" with a first generation swing tag is a rare and valuable find, even though the actual pieces are identical.

IN WHICH AISLE CAN I FIND THE BEANS?

It may seem easy to get lost within the secondary market, but there are many places to turn for direction. You may first want to contact local retailers as they, while not usually involved in the secondary market themselves, are often a great source of information and advice such as how to contact other collectors and where to find swap & sells. By far, the most popular and extensive outlet for the *Beanie Babies* shopper is the Internet. On-line web sites provide an amazing volume of information on every imaginable aspect of the *Beanie Babies* world. There are sites where you can find gossip and news, as well as bulletin boards and chat rooms where you can meet like-minded collectors. You'll also be able to browse auction sites where you can buy and sell.

As the saying goes, *"If it sounds too good to be true, it usually is . . .".* These words ring true when dealing with the secondary market. With this wealth of information comes a wealth of options and the key to being a savvy shopper is to be patient and exercise caution.

"AIN'T NOTHING LIKE THE REAL THING..."

A recent danger in the *Beanie Babies* wilderness is counterfeiting. Always carefully inspect your piece. Pay attention to its material: if it is wrinkled, the wrong color or of inferior quality, you may have a counterfeit. Also, be aware of seam stitching which may not be consistent and ears or eyes which may be out of position or not attached securely. In addition, a counterfeit piece may be understuffed and extremely floppy or over-stuffed and unable to be posed. The pellets inside counterfeit pieces are often cylindrical in shape, not like the round "beans" found in an authentic version.

Tags are also useful in detecting an imitation. Look for the gold foil around the outside edge. Counterfeiters often use a gold colored ink which "bleeds" through to the back. The text on fake tags is often smudged and the edges of the tag are not cleanly cut. Also, minor and often unobserved punctuation details, such as the umlaut (¨) in the word Nürnberg, may be deleted.

THE PRICE OF LOVE

While the secondary market is a thrilling aspect of collecting *Beanie Babies*, it provides no guarantee of returns if you only see collecting as a way to build your fortune. It's up to you to determine your ultimate goal for collecting: you can do it for the investment or for the sheer enjoyment that these plush animals bring.

THE CONDITIONS OF VALUE

Beanie Babies that are in "like-new" condition are the pieces that will command the highest value on the secondary market. First, both the swing tag and the tush tag should be intact. Those that have not been handled (therefore less exposed to risk), as well as those kept in a smoke-free environment also will have a higher value.

Variations

*I*n the world of collectibles, even the slightest of differences between two pieces of the same design can cause quite a stir among collectors. These differences, which may be intentional production changes or old-fashioned mistakes, can be as subtle as a change in the stitching or much more dramatic such as a difference in the overall color or design. And not all differences are to the actual piece itself. Sometimes the piece undergoes a name or tag change. Other common variations are switched swing or tush tags as in the now well-known case of mistaken identity between "Echo" and "Waves."

It is very difficult to predict which of these variations will affect the *Beanie Babies* secondary market value. However, with every change or mistake that each one of these designs undergoes, the alteration makes the piece, as well as the original, special in its own way.

NAME CHANGES

Brownie™/Cubbie™: In his previous life, "Cubbie" was known as "Brownie," one of the "Original Nine" *Beanie Babies* introduced in 1994. Finding this bear with a "Brownie" swing tag is a rare find indeed!

> The Beanie Babies Collection
> **Brownie** ™ style 4010
> © 1993 Ty Inc. Oakbrook, IL. USA
> All Rights Reserved. Caution:
> Remove this tag before giving
> toy to a child. For ages 5 and up.
> Handmade in Korea.
> Surface
> Wash.

> The Beanie Babies Collection
> **Cubbie** ™ style 4010
> © 1993 Ty Inc. Oakbrook, IL. USA
> All Rights Reserved. Caution:
> Remove this tag before giving
> toy to a child. For ages 5 and up.
> Handmade in Korea.
> Surface
> Wash.

Creepy™/Spinner™: Perhaps this arachnid's true personality is showing through with the appearance of the descriptive name "Creepy" on some of its tush tags. Now that "Spinner" has retired, this variation may attract even greater interest.

> The
> Beanie Babies
> Collection®
> ★ **ty** ★
> **Creepy**™
> HAND MADE IN CHINA
> © 1996 TY INC,
> OAKBROOK IL, U.S.A.
> SURFACE WASHABLE
> ALL NEW MATERIAL
> POLYESTER FIBER
> & P.V.C. PELLETS CE
> REG. NO PA. 1965(KR)

> The
> Beanie Babies
> Collection®
> ★ **ty** ★
> **Spinner**™
> HAND MADE IN CHINA
> © 1996 TY INC,
> OAKBROOK IL, U.S.A.
> SURFACE WASHABLE
> ALL NEW MATERIAL
> POLYESTER FIBER
> & P.V.C. PELLETS CE
> REG. NO PA. 1965(KR)

VARIATIONS

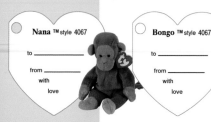

Doodle™/Strut™: In 1997, "Doodle" changed his name to "Strut." Rumor has it that this change in identity came about after a copyright issue with another company.

Nana™/Bongo™: In this first in a series of transformations, "Nana," a tan-tailed monkey, became "Bongo" in 1995.

Pride™/Maple™: This Canadian-exclusive bear was initially named "Pride" and when a last-minute name change to "Maple" occurred, a limited number of "Pride" tags had already been released.

Punchers™/Pinchers™: Released in 1994, some "Pinchers" have been seen sporting first generation swing tags that read "Punchers." Some collectors even say that "Punchers" looks slightly different, with larger, puffier claws and longer, thicker antennas.

Spook™/Spooky™: "Spook" was sighted on tags in late 1995, but was exorcised by "Spooky" within months, never to be seen again!

COLLECTOR'S
VALUE GUIDE™

Tuck™/Tusk™: Some fourth generation swing tags on this walrus display the misspelling "Tuck."

COLOR CHANGES

Digger™: First produced as an orange crustacean, "Digger" eventually turned a bright shade of red to match her red Ty swing tag!

Happy™: This hippo was having a hard time showing his happiness with a drab, gray hide so "Happy" decided to change to a much brighter lavender shade.

Inky™: After becoming permanently attached to his mouth, "Inky" adopted a brighter hue of pink. Before that, this leggy pal lived a tan existence with and without his smile!

Lizzy™: "Lizzy" dazzled her buddies when she turned in her retro, tie-dyed look for a more sophisticated vibrant blue coat with black splotches and a yellow and orange underbelly.

Patti™: Depending on the shade of material that was available on the toymaker's table, "Patti" has appeared in a variety of colors over the years.

Peanut™: They say that elephants never forget but "Peanut" seemed to have forgotten to sport a light blue coat and put a dark one on instead. About 2,000 dark blue elephants were released before they returned to the closet for a change in wardrobe.

DESIGN CHANGES

Bongo™: Although "Bongo" finally decided on a name, he was still unsure of what color his tail should be. He finally decided on a tan one after having sported a brown one for a while.

Derby™: "Derby" decided it was time for a new hair style when he grew his fine mane into a coarse, yarn-like mane. Recently, "Derby" has also been "spotted" with a white star on his forehead.

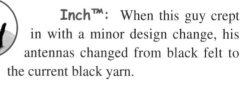

Inch™: When this guy crept in with a minor design change, his antennas changed from black felt to the current black yarn.

Lucky™: Here is a critter who likes to bug us with spotty surprises! First appearing with 7 glued-on spots, "Lucky" later appeared with printed spots that have numbered from 11 to 21.

Magic™: This dramatic dragon's wings took a "hot hiatus" from a pale pink stitching when they donned some hot pink thread. Eventually, "Magic" cooled down and the wings' stitching reverted back to a paler hue.

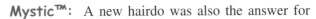

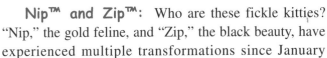

Mystic™: A new hairdo was also the answer for "Mystic" whose mane became coarser over her years of production. And to further mystify collectors, she also acquired a snazzy iridescent horn to replace a tan felt one.

Nip™ and Zip™: Who are these fickle kitties? "Nip," the gold feline, and "Zip," the black beauty, have experienced multiple transformations since January 1995. Initially introduced with white faces and bellies, they changed to solid coats in their respective colors and then found their white boots, which fit so well that they wore them until they were retired.

Quackers™: When first introduced, "Quackers" waddled around without any wings. However, Ty soon realized that a duck without wings is like a fish on a bicycle and redesigned "Quackers" to be more aerodynamically correct.

Rainbow™: What could be the reason for his new pink forked tongue? "Rainbow" might be telling us that he just doesn't care about all of the hoopla concerning the confusion between him and "Iggy."

Sly™: This foxy guy thought he was being sly when he changed the color of his belly from brown to white, but collectors were on to him.

Spot™: Often, a dog's name is a description of its appearance or personality. Not necessarily – as this "Spot" can boldly attest! A spot-less debut caused quite a stir and this pup was soon reintroduced with his namesake on his coat.

Stripes™: This gentle tiger changed his stripes from thick black ones on a dark orange body to thinner ones on a brighter orange body. You might also find a fuzzy belly on some of the darker "Stripes."

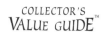

Tank™: This tough little armored "Tank" has put up with a lot of changes in his back "plate" design. He's had seven stitched lines across his back, he's had nine stitched lines across his back and recently, he was 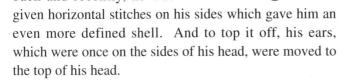 given horizontal stitches on his sides which gave him an even more defined shell. And to top it off, his ears, which were once on the sides of his head, were moved to the top of his head.

Teddy™: These six multi-colored teddy bears, which are some of the more popular of all the *Beanie Babies*, experienced face-lifts to "update" their old-fashioned Victorian bear look. "Teddy" can be found with brown, cranberry, jade, magenta, teal or violet fur.

INTERNAL CHANGES

Princess™: Although many *Beanie Babies* have been produced with both "P.V.C." and "P.E." pellets as noted on the tush tag, collectors of "Princess" covet the earlier "P.V.C." version in particular.

BEANIE BABIES® BIRTHDAYS

JANUARY

Jan. 2, 1998. . . . Zero™
Jan. 3, 1993. . . . Spot™
Jan. 5, 1997. . . . Kuku™
Jan. 6, 1993 . . . Patti™
Jan. 13, 1996. . Crunch™
Jan. 14, 1997. . Spunky™
Jan. 15, 1996 . . . Mel™
Jan. 18, 1994 . . Bones™
Jan. 21, 1996 . . . Nuts™
Jan. 25, 1995. . Peanut™
Jan. 26, 1996 . . . Chip™

FEBRUARY

Feb. 1, 1996 . . . Peace™
Feb. 3, 1998 . . . Beak™
Feb. 4, 1997 . . . Fetch™
Feb. 13, 1995. . . Pinky™
Feb. 13, 1995 . . Stinky™
Feb. 14, 1994 . Valentino™
Feb. 17, 1996 . . Baldy™
Feb. 20, 1996 . . Roary™
Feb. 20, 1997 . . . Early™
Feb. 22, 1995 . . . Tank™
Feb. 25, 1994 . . Happy™
Feb. 27, 1996 . . Sparky™
Feb. 28, 1995 . . . Flip™

MARCH

March 2, 1995 . . Coral™
March 6, 1994 . . . Nip™
March 8, 1996 . Doodle™
March 8, 1996 . . Strut™
March 12, 1997. Rocket™
March 14, 1994 . . Ally™
March 17, 1997 . . Erin™
March 19, 1996. Seaweed™
March 20, 1997. . Early™
March 21, 1996 . Fleece™
March 28, 1994 . . . Zip™
March 29, 1998 . Loosy™

APRIL

April 3, 1996 . . Hoppity™
April 4, 1997 . . . Hissy™
April 5, 1997 . Whisper™
April 7, 1997 . . . . Gigi™
April 12, 1996 . . Curly™
April 16, 1997 . . . Jake™
April 18, 1995 . . . Ears™
April 19, 1994. Quackers™
April 23, 1993. Squealer™
April 25, 1993 . . . Legs™
April 27, 1993. Chocolate™

MAY

May 1, 1995 . . . Lucky™
May 1, 1996 . Wrinkles™
May 2, 1996 . . . Pugsly™
May 3, 1996 . . . Chops™
May 10, 1994 . . . Daisy™
May 11, 1995 . . . Lizzy™
May 13, 1993 . . . Flash™
May 15, 1995 . . . Snort™
May 15, 1995 . Tabasco™
May 19, 1995 . . . Twigs™
May 21, 1994 . . Mystic™
May 28, 1996 . Floppity™
May 29, 1998 . . Canyon™
May 30, 1996 . . . Rover™
May 31, 1997 . . . Wise™

JUNE

June 1, 1996 . . Hippity™
June 3, 1996 . Freckles™
June 3, 1996 . . Scottie™
June 5, 1997 . . Tracker™
June 8, 1995 . . . Bucky™
June 8, 1995 . . Manny™
June 11, 1995 . Stripes™
June 15, 1996 . Scottie™
June 17, 1996 . . Gracie™
June 19, 1993 . Pinchers™
June 27, 1995 . . Bessie™

JULY

July 1, 1996 . . . Maple™
July 1, 1996 . . . Scoop™
July 2, 1995 . . Bubbles™
July 4, 1996 . . . Lefty™
July 4, 1996 . . . Righty™
July 4, 1997 . . . Glory™
July 7, 1998 . . . Clubby™
July 8, 1993 . . . Splash™
July 14, 1995 . . . Ringo™
July 15, 1994 . . Blackie™
July 19, 1995 . . . Grunt™
July 20, 1995 . . Weenie™
July 28, 1996 . Freckles™
July 31, 1998 . . Scorch™

AUGUST

Aug. 1, 1995 . . . Garcia™
Aug. 9, 1995 . . . Hoot™
Aug. 12, 1997 . . . Iggy™
Aug. 13, 1996 . . Spike™
Aug. 14, 1994 . Speedy™
Aug. 17, 1995 . . Bongo™
Aug. 23, 1995 . . Digger™
Aug. 27, 1995 . . . Sting™
Aug. 28, 1997 . . Pounce™
Aug. 31, 1998 . . . Halo™

SEPTEMBER

Sept. 3, 1995 . . . Inch™
Sept. 3, 1996 . . Claude™
Sept. 5, 1995 . . Magic™
Sept. 9, 1997 . . Bruno™
Sept. 12, 1996 . . . Sly™
Sept. 16, 1995 . Derby™
Sept. 16, 1995 . . . Kiwi™
Sept. 18, 1995 . . Tusk™
Sept. 21, 1997 Stretch™
Sept. 27, 1998 . . Roam™
Sept. 29, 1997 . Stinger™

OCTOBER

Oct. 1, 1997 . Smoochy™
Oct. 3, 1996 . . . Bernie™
Oct. 9, 1996 . . . Doby™
Oct. 10, 1997 . Jabber™
Oct. 12, 1996 . . Tuffy™
Oct. 14, 1997 . Rainbow™
Oct. 16, 1995 . Bumble™
Oct. 17, 1996 . . Dotty™
Oct. 22, 1996 . . . Snip™
Oct. 28, 1996 . Spinner™
Oct. 29, 1996 . . Batty™
Oct. 30, 1995 . . Radar™
Oct. 31, 1995 . Spooky™
Oct. 31, 1998 . Pumkin™

NOVEMBER

Nov. 3, 1997 . . Puffer™
Nov. 6, 1996 . . . Pouch™
Nov. 7, 1997 . . . Ants™
Nov. 9, 1996 . . . Congo™
Nov. 14, 1993 . . Cubbie™
Nov. 14, 1994 . . Goldie™
Nov. 20, 1997 . . Prance™
Nov. 21, 1996 . Nanook™
Nov. 27, 1996 . Gobbles™
Nov. 28, 1995 . . Teddy™
(brown)
Nov. 29, 1994 . . . Inky™

DECEMBER

Dec. 2, 1996 . . . Jolly™
Dec. 6, 1997 . . Fortune™
Dec. 6, 1998 . . . Santa™
Dec. 8, 1996 . . Waves™
Dec. 12, 1996 . Blizzard™
Dec. 14, 1996. Seamore™
Dec. 15, 1997. Britannia™
Dec. 16, 1995 . . Velvet™
Dec. 19, 1995 . Waddle™
Dec. 21, 1996 . . . Echo™
Dec. 22, 1996. Snowball™
Dec. 24, 1995 . . Ziggy™
Dec. 25, 1996. '97 Teddy™
Dec. 25, 1998. '98 Teddy™

WORD SEARCH

Find your favorite *Beanie Babies®* in this challenging word search.
There are 17 in all. Happy hunting! *(See page 140 for answers).*

BRONTY™
DERBY™
ERIN™
FLEECE™
GARCIA™
GLORY™
INCH™
JAKE™
LUCKY™
MAPLE™
NANA™
RINGO™
SNOWBALL™
SPARKY™
STEG™
VALENTINO™
WADDLE™

```
A S N O W B A L L B C D
E F M L B R O N T Y G H
I J K A L M N S O P R Q
R D S G P T U P T V I W
X Y E A L L Z A A E N B
C W D R E O E R F G G H
I A J C B K R K L M O N
O D P I Q Y R Y S T U V
F D V A L E N T I N O B
W L X Y Z U A A B C D E
F E E G H I C J N J K L
M N R E O P Q K R A S T
U V I N C H Y W Y K X Y
Z A N B C D E F E G H
```

WORD SCRAMBLE

Rearrange the letters to spell your favorite *Beanie Babies®* names.
The white snowballs spell out a secret *Beanie Babies®* name.
Good luck! *(See page 140 for answers).*

1. RKWSNIEL
2. PIOYLTPF
3. ZALIRDZB
4. ECEPA
5. BTSAACO
6. HPOCU
7. IYTIPHP

Keep your
heads up
or in this case down.
When we play hide-and-seek,
I'm the best hider around.
Who am I?

PICTURE FUN: BEAK™ TO THE RESCUE
Use the pictures on the right to help finish the story!
(See page 140 for answers).

One day, after a ▢+y winter storm, 🐧 and the other *Beanie Babies* decided to go

▢+ing. They were having a good time, when 🐧 noticed 🦤 was by himself,

crying. "Why are you sad?" asked 🐧. "I want to be like the other ▢+s," said

🦤. "I can't fly, and I have this long funny-looking ▢." 🐧 tried to cheer up

🦤. He told all the funny ▢ and jokes he knew. But 🦤 was still ▢.

Suddenly, there was a loud ▢ and a lot of yelling and splashing. 🐕 had fallen in the

▢! 🐧 and 🦤 ran to where 🐕 was shivering. 🦤 leaned over to

🐕 and yelled, "Grab onto my beak and I'll pull you out!" 🦤 pulled 🐕 out

of the water as the other *Beanie Babies* cheered. They all went ▢ for some ▢ and

🦤 and the rest of the *Beanie Babies* played games until it was time for bed.

TRIVIA QUIZ
Test your knowledge of *Beanie Babies®* facts here!
(See page 140 for answers).

1. Which Women's National Basketball Association teams featured Sports Promotion *Beanie Babies* in 1998?

2. Which of the *Beanie Buddies* was introduced at the same time as his *Beanie Babies* counterpart?

3. According to his poem, which *Beanie Babies* animal eats broccoli and cheese?

4. How many *Beanie Babies* are wearing hats? Name them.

5. What world traveling bear was only offered in Great Britain?

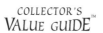

On this handy list, you can check off which Beanie Babies are in your collection. You can also circle the numbered heart that corresponds with the tag generation that your Beanie Babies animal is wearing.

Current Beanie Babies®

- ☐ 1998 Holiday Teddy™ .. ❺
- ☐ Ants™ .... ❺
- ☐ Batty™ .... ❹ ❺
- ☐ Beak™ .... ❺
- ☐ Bongo™ (tan tail). ❸ ❹ ❺
- ☐ Britannia™ .... ❺
- ☐ Canyon™ .... ❺
- ☐ Chip™ .... ❹ ❺
- ☐ Chocolate™. ❶ ❷ ❸ ❹ ❺
- ☐ Claude™ .... ❹ ❺
- ☐ Clubby™ .... ❺
- ☐ Congo™ .... ❹ ❺
- ☐ Curly™ .... ❹ ❺
- ☐ Derby™ (star) .... ❺
- ☐ Doby™ .... ❹ ❺
- ☐ Dotty™ .... ❹ ❺
- ☐ Early™ .... ❺
- ☐ Erin™ .... ❺
- ☐ Fetch™ .... ❺
- ☐ Fleece™ .... ❹ ❺
- ☐ Fortune™ .... ❺
- ☐ Freckles™ .... ❹ ❺
- ☐ Gigi™ .... ❺
- ☐ Glory™ .... ❺
- ☐ Gobbles™ .... ❹ ❺
- ☐ Halo™ .... ❺
- ☐ Hissy™ .... ❺
- ☐ Iggy™ .... ❺
- ☐ Jabber™ .... ❺
- ☐ Jake™ .... ❺
- ☐ Kuku™ .... ❺
- ☐ Loosy™ .... ❺
- ☐ Maple™
  ("Maple™" tush tag). ❹ ❺
- ☐ Mel™ .... ❹ ❺
- ☐ Mystic™
  (iridescent horn) ... ❹ ❺
- ☐ Nanook™ .... ❹ ❺
- ☐ Nuts™ .... ❹ ❺

- ☐ Peace™ .... ❹ ❺
- ☐ Pinky™ .... ❸ ❹ ❺
- ☐ Pouch™ .... ❹ ❺
- ☐ Pounce™ .... ❺
- ☐ Prance™ .... ❺
- ☐ Princess™ (P.E. pellets) . ❹
- ☐ Pugsly™ .... ❹ ❺
- ☐ Pumkin'™ .... ❺
- ☐ Rainbow™ (tongue) ..... ❺
- ☐ Roam™ .... ❺
- ☐ Roary™ .... ❹ ❺
- ☐ Rocket™ .... ❺
- ☐ Santa™ .... ❺
- ☐ Scoop™ .... ❹ ❺
- ☐ Scorch™ .... ❺
- ☐ Smoochy™ .... ❺
- ☐ Snip™ .... ❹ ❺
- ☐ Spike™ .... ❹ ❺
- ☐ Spunky™ .... ❺
- ☐ Stinger™ .... ❺
- ☐ Stretch™ .... ❺
- ☐ Strut™ .... ❹ ❺
- ☐ Tracker™ .... ❺
- ☐ Tuffy™ .... ❹ ❺
- ☐ Valentino™ ... ❷ ❸ ❹ ❺
- ☐ Whisper™ .... ❺
- ☐ Wise™ .... ❺
- ☐ Zero™ .... ❺

Retired Beanie Babies®

- ☐ 1997 Teddy™ .... ❹
- ☐ Ally™ .... ❶ ❷ ❸ ❹
- ☐ Baldy™ .... ❹ ❺
- ☐ Bernie™ .... ❹ ❺
- ☐ Bessie™ .... ❸ ❹
- ☐ Billionaire™ .... **Special Tag**
- ☐ Blackie™... ❶ ❷ ❸ ❹ ❺
- ☐ Blizzard™ .... ❹ ❺
- ☐ Bones™ ... ❶ ❷ ❸ ❹ ❺
- ☐ Bronty™ .... ❸
- ☐ Brownie™ .... ❶
- ☐ Bruno™ .... ❺
- ☐ Bubbles™ .... ❸ ❹
- ☐ Bucky™ .... ❸ ❹
- ☐ Bumble™ .... ❸ ❹
- ☐ Caw™ .... ❸
- ☐ Chilly™ .... ❶ ❷ ❸
- ☐ Chops™ .... ❸ ❹
- ☐ Coral™ .... ❸ ❹

- ☐ Crunch™ .... ❹ ❺
- ☐ Cubbie™ .. ❶ ❷ ❸ ❹ ❺
- ☐ Daisy™ .... ❶ ❷ ❸ ❹ ❺
- ☐ Derby™
  (coarse mane) ...... ❸ ❹
- ☐ Derby™
  (fine mane) .... ❸
- ☐ Digger™ (red) ...... ❸ ❹
- ☐ Digger™ (orange). ❶ ❷ ❸
- ☐ Doodle™ .... ❹
- ☐ Ears™ .... ❸ ❹ ❺
- ☐ Echo™ .... ❹ ❺
- ☐ Flash™ .... ❶ ❷ ❸ ❹
- ☐ Flip™ .... ❸ ❹
- ☐ Floppity™ .... ❹ ❺
- ☐ Flutter™ .... ❸
- ☐ Garcia™ .... ❸ ❹
- ☐ Goldie™ ... ❶ ❷ ❸ ❹ ❺
- ☐ Gracie™ .... ❹ ❺
- ☐ Grunt™ .... ❸ ❹
- ☐ Happy™ (lavender). ❸ ❹ ❺
- ☐ Happy™ (gray) ... ❶ ❷ ❸
- ☐ Hippity™ .... ❹ ❺
- ☐ Hoot™ .... ❸ ❹
- ☐ Hoppity™ .... ❹ ❺
- ☐ Humphrey™ ..... ❶ ❷ ❸
- ☐ Inch™
  (yarn antennas).... ❹ ❺
- ☐ Inch™
  (felt antennas)..... ❸ ❹
- ☐ Inky™ (pink).... ❸ ❹ ❺
- ☐ Inky™
  (tan with mouth).... ❷ ❸
- ☐ Inky™
  (tan without mouth). ❶ ❷
- ☐ Jolly™ .... ❹ ❺
- ☐ Kiwi™ .... ❸ ❹
- ☐ Lefty™ .... ❹
- ☐ Legs™ .... ❶ ❷ ❸ ❹
- ☐ Libearty™ .... ❹
- ☐ Lizzy™ (blue) .... ❸ ❹ ❺
- ☐ Lizzy™ (tie-dye) .... ❸
- ☐ Lucky™ (11 spots) .. ❹ ❺
- ☐ Lucky™ (21 spots)...... ❹
- ☐ Lucky™ (7 spots). ❶ ❷ ❸
- ☐ Magic™
  (pale pink thread) .. ❸ ❹
- ☐ Magic™
  (hot pink thread)...... ❹
- ☐ Manny™ .... ❸ ❹

- ❏ Maple™ ("Pride™" tush tag) ..... ❹
- ❏ Mystic™ (brown horn/ coarse mane) .... ❸ ❹
- ❏ Mystic™ (brown horn/ fine mane) ...... ❶ ❷ ❸
- ❏ Nana™ .... ❸
- ❏ Nip™ (white paws) . ❸ ❹ ❺
- ❏ Nip™ (all gold) .... ❸
- ❏ Nip™ (white face) ... ❷ ❸
- ❏ Patti™ (magenta) . ❸ ❹ ❺
- ❏ Patti™ (maroon) .. ❶ ❷ ❸
- ❏ Peanut™ (light blue) . ❸ ❹ ❺
- ❏ Peanut™ (dark blue) .... ❸
- ❏ Peking™ .... ❶ ❷ ❸
- ❏ Pinchers™ ("Pinchers™" swing tag) . ❶ ❷ ❸ ❹ ❺
- ❏ Pinchers™ ("Punchers™" swing tag) .... ❶
- ❏ Princess™ (P.V.C. pellets) .... ❹
- ❏ Puffer™ .... ❺
- ❏ Quackers™ ("Quackers™" with wings) ... ❷ ❸ ❹ ❺
- ❏ Quackers™ ("Quacker™" without wings) ..... ❶ ❷
- ❏ Radar™ .... ❸ ❹
- ❏ Rainbow™ (no tongue) .. ❺
- ❏ Rex™ .... ❸
- ❏ Righty™ .... ❹
- ❏ Ringo™ .... ❸ ❹ ❺
- ❏ Rover™ .... ❹ ❺
- ❏ Scottie™ .... ❹ ❺
- ❏ Seamore™ .... ❶ ❷ ❸ ❹
- ❏ Seaweed™ .... ❸ ❹ ❺
- ❏ Slither™ .... ❶ ❷ ❸
- ❏ Sly™ (white belly) ... ❹ ❺
- ❏ Sly™ (brown belly) ..... ❹
- ❏ Snort™ .... ❹
- ❏ Snowball™ .... ❹
- ❏ Sparky™ .... ❹
- ❏ Speedy™ ..... ❶ ❷ ❸ ❹
- ❏ Spinner™ ("Spinner™" tush tag) .... ❹ ❺
- ❏ Spinner™ ("Creepy™" tush tag) .... ❺
- ❏ Splash™ ...... ❶ ❷ ❸ ❹
- ❏ Spooky™ ("Spooky™" swing tag) .... ❸ ❹

- ❏ Spooky™ ("Spook™" swing tag) .... ❸
- ❏ Spot™ (with spot) . ❷ ❸ ❹
- ❏ Spot™ (without spot) . ❶ ❷
- ❏ Squealer™ . ❶ ❷ ❸ ❹ ❺
- ❏ Steg™ .... ❸
- ❏ Sting™ .... ❸ ❹
- ❏ Stinky™ .... ❸ ❹ ❺
- ❏ Stripes™ (light w/fewer stripes) ... ❹ ❺
- ❏ Stripes™ (dark w/fuzzy belly) .... ❸
- ❏ Stripes™ (dark w/more stripes) .... ❸
- ❏ Tabasco™ .... ❸ ❹
- ❏ Tank™ (9 plates/with shell) ... ❹
- ❏ Tank™ (9 plates/without shell) . ❹
- ❏ Tank™ (7 plates/without shell) . ❸
- ❏ Teddy™ (brown, new face) .... ❷ ❸ ❹
- ❏ Teddy™ (brown, old face) .... ❶ ❷
- ❏ Teddy™ (cranberry, new face) .... ❷ ❸
- ❏ Teddy™ (cranberry, old face) .... ❶ ❷
- ❏ Teddy™ (jade, new face) .... ❷ ❸
- ❏ Teddy™ (jade, old face) .... ❶ ❷
- ❏ Teddy™ (magenta, new face) .... ❷ ❸
- ❏ Teddy™ (magenta, old face) .... ❶ ❷
- ❏ Teddy™ (teal, new face) .... ❷ ❸
- ❏ Teddy™ (teal, old face) ..... ❶ ❷
- ❏ Teddy™ (violet, new face) ... ❷ ❸
- ❏ Teddy™ (violet, new face/ employee bear w/red tush tag) ... **No Swing Tag**
- ❏ Teddy™ (violet, old face) ... ❶ ❷
- ❏ Trap™ .... ❶ ❷ ❸

- ❏ Tusk™ ("Tusk™" swing tag) . ❸ ❹
- ❏ Tusk™ ("Tuck™" swing tag) .... ❹
- ❏ Twigs™ .... ❸ ❹ ❺
- ❏ Velvet™ .... ❸ ❹
- ❏ Waddle™ .... ❸ ❹ ❺
- ❏ Waves™ .... ❹ ❺
- ❏ Web™ .... ❶ ❷ ❸
- ❏ Weenie™ .... ❸ ❹ ❺
- ❏ Wrinkles™ .... ❹ ❺
- ❏ Ziggy™ .... ❸ ❹ ❺
- ❏ Zip™ (white paws) . ❸ ❹ ❺
- ❏ Zip™ (all black) .... ❸
- ❏ Zip™ (white face) ... ❷ ❸

Beanie Buddies®

- ❏ Beak™
- ❏ Humphrey™
- ❏ Jake™
- ❏ Peanut™
- ❏ Quackers™
- ❏ Rover™
- ❏ Stretch™
- ❏ Teddy™
- ❏ Twigs™

Teenie Beanie Babies™

- ❏ 1997 Teenie Beanie Babies™ Complete Set
- ❏ 1998 Teenie Beanie Babies™ Complete Set
- ❏ Bones™
- ❏ Bongo™
- ❏ Chocolate™
- ❏ Chops™
- ❏ Doby™
- ❏ Goldie™
- ❏ Happy™
- ❏ Inch™
- ❏ Lizz™
- ❏ Mel™
- ❏ Patti™
- ❏ Peanut™
- ❏ Pinchers™
- ❏ Pinky™
- ❏ Quacks™
- ❏ Scoop™
- ❏ Seamore™
- ❏ Snort™
- ❏ Speedy™
- ❏ Twigs™
- ❏ Waddle™
- ❏ Zip™

(BD) = Beanie Buddies®

(TB) = Teenie Beanie Babies™

ALPHABETICAL INDEX

Below is an alphabetical listing of the Beanie Babies and the pages you can find them on in the Value Guide!

GAMES ANSWERS
WORD SEARCH

WORD SCRAMBLE

1. Wrinkles™   5. Tabasco™
2. Floppity™   6. Pouch™
3. Blizzard™   7. Hippity™
4. Peace™

SECRET: Stretch™

PICTURE FUN

1. snow   6. sad
2. ice skate   7. crack
3. bird   8. water
4. beak   9. home
5. stories   10. hot cocoa

TRIVIA QUIZ

1. Charlotte Sting, . Cleveland Rockers, Detroit Shock, Houston Comets, Los Angeles Sparks, Washington Mystics
2. Beak™
3. Cubbie™
4. Six – 1997 Teddy™, 1998 Holiday Teddy™, Santa™, Snowball™, Wise™, Zero™
5. Britannia™

Collectors' Publishing Presents The

*T*n January, Collectors' Publishing launched the Dream Beanie Contest and the responses have been pouring in. Every month, three winners are selected and those winners can be found posted on our web site (*www.collectorspub.com*). The winners from June, July, August and September can also be found on the following pages.

To enter is easy, all you need is a bit of imagination.

PICK A NAME!
CREATE A BIRTHDATE!
WRITE A POEM!
DRAW A PICTURE!

SEND YOUR ENTRY TO:
Collectors' Publishing
P.O. Box 2333
Meriden, CT 06450

You can find official entry forms on the web site, but you better act fast as time is running out. By December 1998, the contest will be over!

No purchase necessary. All submissions become the property of Collectors' Publishing. Collectors' Publishing is not affiliated with Ty Inc. and winning designs will not be produced by Ty. Winners will be selected by the Collectors' Publishing staff. Due to the volume of entries, we cannot respond to all entries and submissions are not returnable. All entries must be postmarked no later than December 31, 1998. For a list of winners, write to Collectors' Publishing, Attn: Contest Winners, P.O. Box 2333, Meriden, CT 06450 or check our web site. Void where prohibited by law.

www.collectorspub.com

Dream Beanie Contest Winners

JUNE

"Twinkle" the Starfish
Birthday: April
By: John T. & Beth T., Waco, TX

1ST PLACE

Stranded on the beach at sea,
A starfish dies if left to be.
You can save this one today,
By giving him love and a place to stay.

"Old Smokey" the Burro
Birthday: October 7, 1998
By: Lauren N., Mt. Laurel, NJ

2ND PLACE

Old Smokey roams the wild west,
He walks all day without a rest.
His cute little hat protects him from the sun,
But with his hat he can never tell when the day is done!

"Stringy" the Jellyfish
Birthday: November 13, 1998
By: Emily P., Longwood, FL

3RD PLACE

I play in the waves,
It makes me sort of dingy.
I have long legs,
That's why they call me stringy.

JULY

"Willy" the Wasp
Birthday: June 26, 1998
By: Kevin S., Johnson, NE

1ST PLACE

Willy the wasp loves to have fun,
Buzzing and flying is what he has done.
You may be afraid he will try to sting,
But please don't run, he won't hurt a thing.

"Howl" the Tie-Dyed Wolf
Birthday: September 19, 1998
By: Briana A., Queens Village, NY

2ND PLACE

Howling is what she likes to do,
Be very careful she will howl at you.
Look at her cute puppy dog face,
When she walks she walks with grace.

"Hammy" the Hamster
Birthday: May 2, 1998
By: Renee H., Westminster, CA

3RD PLACE

Hammy the hamster sleeps all day,
At night he wants to eat and play.
Hammy likes to run on his wheel,
After that he eats his meal.

DREAM BEANIE CONTEST WINNERS

AUGUST

"Puffy" the Blowfish
Birthday: July 27, 1998
By: Jennifer N., Margate, NJ

1ST PLACE

Puffy the blowfish lives under the sea,
Swimming along with his best friend Goldie.
When a shark comes by in the night,
He puffs up and away goes his fright.

"Charlie" the Cougar
Birthday: October 7, 1998
By: Laura Jean W., Palm Springs, CA

2ND PLACE

Up in the mountains he hunts his prey,
That's what he does every day.
He finds shelter in his cave,
Where he dreams of being brave.

"Vic" the Lemur
Birthday: June 26
By: Gloria K., Lawrenceville, GA

3RD PLACE

Vic the lemur loves to play,
Sometimes hide or run away.
But soon you'll hear a loud shriek!
He's only playing hide and seek.

SEPTEMBER

"Nibbles" the Goat
Birthday: September 22, 1997
By: Alle W., Dana Point, CA

1ST PLACE

Nibbles is one hungry goat,
He eats to help his furry coat.
He'll chop on anything in sight,
But give him a hug and he won't bite!

"Wiley" the Big, Wild Cat
Birthday: April 22, 1998
By: Dolly V., Mattoon, IL

2ND PLACE

Wiley is a big cat: unlike any other.
Passing down the generation, just like his mother.
Looking different, he thinks, is the best,
Because he stands out better than the rest.

"Simon" the Sea Monster
Birthday: January 27, 1998
By: Debbie P., Palmdale, CA

3RD PLACE

Swimming and playing in the sea,
Makes Simon happy as can be.
You see he's a sea monster living under a pier,
But he's just so sweet there's nothing to fear.

Cherished Teddies®
by ENESCO®

Department 56®
Villages

HALLMARK
Keepsake Ornaments

by ENESCO

Ty® Beanie Babies®

Department 56®
Snowbabies™

Puffkins®

SWAROVSKI
Silver Crystal

Ty® Plush Animals

Look for these other

COLLECTOR'S
VALUE GUIDE™

titles at fine gift and
collectible stores everywhere.

14 Collectible Titles

Featuring

- **What's New**
- **Full-Color Photos Of Every Piece**
- Up-To-Date Secondary Market Values
- Easy-To-Use Indexes

TY® BEANIE BABIES®	DEPT. 56® VILLAGES
TY® PLUSH ANIMALS	DREAMSICLES™
BOYDS PLUSH ANIMALS	HALLMARK ORNAMENTS
BOYDS RESIN FIGURINES	HARBOUR LIGHTS®
CHARMING TAILS®	PRECIOUS MOMENTS®
CHERISHED TEDDIES®	PUFFKINS®
DEPT. 56® SNOWBABIES™	SWAROVSKI CRYSTAL

COLLECTORS' PUBLISHING

598 Pomeroy Avenue · Meriden, CT 06450

www.collectorspub.com
(check out our web site's exciting new look coming in December 1998)